VIRGIL THOMSON'S MUSICAL PORTRAITS

Virgil Thomson, c. 1928, the year he composed his first musical portrait; photo by Man Ray, copyright, Juliet Man Ray, 1985. (From the collection of Virgil Thomson.)

ANTHONY TOMMASINI

VIRGIL THOMSON'S MUSICAL PORTRAITS

Preface by
VIRGIL THOMSON

THEMATIC CATALOGUES No. 13

PENDRAGON PRESS
NEW YORK

THEMATIC CATALOGUE SERIES

Library of Congress Cataloging-in-Publication Data

Tommasini, Anthony C.
   Virgil Thomson's musical portraits

   (Thematic Catalogues ; no. 13
   1. Thomson, Virgil, 1896;   Instrumental
music.   I. Title.   2. Series.
ML410.T452T6   1986   780'.92'4   85-6297
ISBN 0-918728-51-7

Table of Contents

PART I: MUSICAL PORTRAITURE

PART II: A THEMATIC CATALOGUE

PART I

MUSICAL PORTRAITURE

The author gratefully acknowledges permission to reprint excerpts from the following:

Virgil Thomson, by Virgil Thomson, copyright © 1966 by Virgil Thomson. Reprinted by permission of Alfred A. Knopf, Inc.
The Virgil Thomson Reader, by Virgil Thomson. Copyright © 1981 by Virgil Thomson. First published in "John Rockwell: A Conversation with Virgil Thomson", *Parnassus: Poetry in Review*, Spring/Summer, 1977. Reprinted by permission of Houghton Mifflin Company.
"Of Portraits and Operas" by Virgil Thomson, from *Antaeus* 21/22 (Spring/Summer, 1976), 208-210. Reprinted by permission of *Antaeus*.
Out of This Century: Confessions of An Art Addict, by Peggy Guggenheim, copyright © 1979 by Peggy Guggenheim. Reprinted by permission of Universe Books.
"Preface" by Lincoln Kirstein to *Essays and Criticisms of Henry McBride; Selected, with an Introduction by Daniel Catton Rich*, copyright © 1975 by Daniel Catton Rich. Reprinted by permission of Atheneum Publishers.
Picasso: His Life and Work, by Roland Penrose, copyright © 1959 by Roland Penrose. Reprinted by permission of Harper and Row Publishers.
"Alternations: A Portrait of Maurice Grosser" from *Portraits for Piano Solo, Album One* by Virgil Thomson. Copyright © 1948 Mercury Music, reassigned to Virgil Thomson 1969. Used by permission of publisher, G. Schirmer, Inc.
"In a Bird Cage: A Portrait of Lise Deharme" from *Portraits for Piano Solo, Album Two* by Virgil Thomson. Copyright © 1949 Mercury Music, reassigned to Virgil Thomson 1969. Used by permission of publisher, G. Schirmer, Inc.
"Florine Stettheimer: Parades" from *Thirteen Portraits for Piano* (1981), by Virgil Thomson. Copyright © 1981 by Virgil Thomson. Reprinted by permission of Boosey & Hawkes, Inc., Sole Agents.
"Richard Flender: Solid, Not Stolid" from *Nineteen Portraits for Piano* (1981), by Virgil Thomson. Copyright © 1981 by Virgil Thomson. Reprinted by permission of Boosey & Hawkes, Inc. Sole Agents.

Preface

by Virgil Thomson

Of making musical portraits I do not know the beginning, and certainly for now there is no predictable end.

Neither has its essential methodology changed. The format can be anything known to music—song shapes such as ABA and the like, dance-meters, rondos, sonata-forms, and all the non-repeating continuities.

Their textures can be monolinear or multichordal, canonic, fugal, melodic with oom-pah, harmonious, discordant, twelve-tonish, percussive, or merely noise. Any instrument or any combo will do, any kind of sound, loud or tranquil, familiar or surprising.

The expressive content can vary too; indeed it must, since the subject is one person, or at most a group of related individuals. And here is where the problem of resemblance comes up.

The relation of any music to its subject is a composer's choice. Raindrops, bugle calls, bells, a limping gait—all these are easy to suggest. Their value to characterization, however, can only be metaphorical. And metaphor in music is easiest to hear when the music itself recalls other music, or at the very least some kind of sound. A verbal connection is harder for the listener to pick up, and visual image such as colors or forms is virtually impossible to communicate through the ear. Perfumes and stenches, sweet tastes and the sour, are a bit easier, though they may need a program note.

Emotional and temperamental characteristics, all the things we perceive by empathy, are natural, for music is the language of the feelings. The more spontaneously they are expressed the more convincingly received. The less hindered by the verbal or the vision the more intensely they can penetrate as a musical experience.

Actually it was in search of such immediacy that I began making musical portraits as a painter works, in the model's presence. This led me toward seeking ways to keep my work spontaneous, the music flowing out of me unhindered by thoughts, at least by verbalizings. I called this trick "letting my mind alone", or later and more pretentiously "the discipline of spontaneity". For indeed it is a discipline and not unlike that which the religious practice in search of self-containment, its aim a ready-for-anything passivity which can allow things to happen. Portraiture itself has also a parallel in psychotherapy, where an intimacy between doctor and patient can produce a state of mutual trust called the "transference".

I think I am the first of the portrait composers to use an artist-and-model intimacy as my working method. I have found it a fecund one, since according to Tommasini, my portraits now number 140, and I think not more than a dozen of these were composed away from the model.

Another benefit of direct action is that I do not have to know the sitter; I can sketch a stranger as well as an old friend, anyone in fact except those who resist me. The sitter who will not let go cannot, as any painter knows, be portrayed with sympathy. Cartooned yes, but in that emergency I tend to abandon the whole enterprise.

As for verification of a resemblance, the large variety of styles and formats that can be found among my portraits is something beyond merely musical evidence. Also persons acquainted with the sitters not infrequently recognize characteristics. There is no test for any of this, however, comparable to the recognition of colors and forms and personalities that is common with visual portraiture.

The portrait in music, no matter how spontaneously composed, is program-music no less than is landscape depiction or following a verbal story. Any starting point, external to oneself or introspective, is fine for setting off the imagination, but nothing can take the place of a good musical idea. And what is a musical idea? It is the juxtaposition of two or more musical motifs or situations, any two; but a good musical idea is usually one which bears some element, however slight, of strangeness, of surprise. And a good musical piece is definable as one that can hold the attention of persons accustomed to having their attention held by music's own continuities. Whatever happens to precede this is for the composer a jumping off place, a diving board.

Music in the long run tends for musicians to be just music. But very little has ever been written down that the author did not think was about something. Some thing or some body. So every musical portrait is tied to an individual, and the composer of it tends to believe it a true likeness. He hopes it will also be good music.

Acknowledgments

For their assistance and advice in preparing this book for publication I wish to acknowledge the following individuals: from the Boston University School of Music Faculty, Dr. Karol Berger (now at Stanford), Mr. Charles Fussell, and Dr. Maria Clodes; from Emerson College in Boston, my associates Leslie Schneider, Kevin Miller, and June La Pointe; from the Vassar College Art Gallery, Sally Mills; from the Vassar College Music Library, Sabrina L. Weiss; from the Beinecke Rare Book and Manuscript Library at Yale University, Mr. Donald Gallup and Mr. David Schoonover; from the Yale School of Music Library, Mr. Victor Cardell, and Ms. Kathleen J. Moretto; from the Yale School of Drama, Dr. Leon Katz; and from the Yale School of Music, Professor Donald Currier and his wife Charlotte, providers of housing, food, and friendship during many days of New Haven-based research.

In researching this book I contacted virtually all of the living subjects of the Thomson portraits—the "still-available sitters," as Virgil Thomson has put it—as well as the friends and relations of other sitters now deceased. Many of these individuals are devoted friends of Virgil Thomson and their responses to my requests for aid were very gratifying. For their generous contributions—letters, information, photographs, art work, telephone calls—I wish to thank the following: Ms. Joell Amar and Dr. Benjamin Zifkin, Pamela Askew, Franco Assetto and Ms. Betty Freeman, Sarah Goodwin Austin, Maurice Bavoux, Christopher Beach, Power Boothe, Paul Bowles, Briggs W. Buchanan, Gerald Busby, Samuel Byers, Philip Claflin,

Christopher Cox, Noah Creshevsky, Molly Davies, David Dubal, Anne S. Fuller, Charles Fussell, Morris Golde, Louise Hastings, Henry-Russell Hitchcock, John Houseman, Germaine Hugnet, Frederic James, Bufffie Johnson, Theodate Johnson, Cynthia Kemper, Danyal Lawson, Brendan Lemon, Bennett Lerner, Rodney Lister, Madame Man Ray, Malitte Matta, Peter McWilliams, Phillip Ramey, Dr. Marcel Roche and D̃ona Flor, Jay Rozen, Craig Rutenberg, Paul Sanfançon, Anne-Marie Soullière, Flavie Alvarez de Toledo, and Dr. Fred Tulan.

Very special thanks go to Mr. Maurice Grosser for his help, support, and his generous permission to reprint several photos of his handsome paintings; Mr. Louis Rispoli, Virgil Thomson's excellent and cheerful secretary, for his extensive assistance, and permission to quote his lengthy essay on his working relationship with Thomson; and Mr. Scott Wheeler, my friend and colleague who introduced me to Virgil Thomson.

Because of his generous assistance and his contributions to the research and writing of this work, Mr. Virgil Thomson has assured its lasting value and won my inexpressible gratitude. Documents, manuscripts, correspondences—all were made available to me. The circumstances of my "hard research" could not have been more engaging and pleasant: hours of recorded formal interviews, hours of informal conversations—over a hearty meal at his Chelsea suite, over Italian fare at my Brookline apartment—and several exciting coaching sessions of my piano performances. Virgil Thomson's recall of detail and incident assured that I could "get it right," as he put it. For example: "Virgil, you composed portraits of Ettie and Carrie Stettheimer on the same day, May 5, 1935. Do you remember whom you sketched first?" He did.

For his Preface, his editorial assistance, his generosity, his goodwill, and for his wonderful musical portraits, I am greatly indebted to Virgil Thomson.

Anthony Tommasini
Brookline, Massachusetts
March, 1985

CHAPTER 1

Introduction: What is a "Musical Portrait?"

Vladimir Nabokov once answered a critic's speculation on the meaning of his novel *Lolita* by offering his own interpretation: *"Lolita* is a record of my love affair with the English language." This answer illustrates the reticence with which many artists and critics tackle all questions concerning the expressive meaning of art, especially in the twentieth century. Indeed, it has been argued that all art is ultimately about its own formal aesthetic components and is largely self-referential. No one would disagree, least of all Nabokov, that *Lolita* is also about the nature of obsessive sexual desire. But like many artists of his stature, Nabokov left the specifics of these discussions to others. Perhaps—for this, his first novel in English—Nabokov simply contrived a narrative that would be powerful enough to serve him as an effective venue for his brilliant use of the English language.

When the debate about the meaning and expressive domain of art is applied to music, especially purely instrumental music, the issues become even more intractable. Music communicates its expressive content with a subliminal power that is at once immediate, yet largely inarticulate. Similarly, the form and structure of music—which is presented with such narrative, sequential clarity—remains elusive to most listeners, at least until repeated hearings. (I am discussing so-called "absolute" instrumental music. All music which sets a text must be discussed in conjunction with its text; vocal and dramatic music raise quite separate aesthetic issues.)

What can music express? Some twentieth century musicians, Stravinsky among them, try to argue that music can express nothing other than commentary upon itself or other music. Stravinsky's music from his neo-Classic period is sometimes described as music about older music. It could be argued that even so seemingly "meaningful" a piece as Messiaen's *Quartet for the End of Time* is more about Rhythm than it is about Eternity. But one musical genre for which this viewpoint presents special difficulties is the abstract musical portrait.

The word "portrait" commonly denotes the representation of a person in a visual medium, and it is, of course, the arts of painting and drawing that have the richest heritage of portraiture. Only in the most figurative sense of the term can the word "portrait" even be applied to a representation or likeness other than a visual one. (The abstract "literary portrait" as practiced by Gertrude Stein, we shall see, is not simply a literary description of a character, but a unique genre.) Yet, when an artistic work is called a portrait it is assumed that the expressive content is quite explicit—namely, the artistic depiction of a specific individual or group. I raise these familiar questions not to answer them, but to apply them to the subject of this study, the musical portrait.

As practiced by Virgil Thomson, the musical portrait attempts to do the seemingly impossible—to depict in an abstract instrumental composition the inner nature of the portrait subject. There is a rich history in music of pieces sometimes called portraits that are, in fact, merely compositions dedicated to, in homage to, or inspired by their subjects. There is a more meager tradition of portraits that attempt to literally and specifically depict character in music. Thomson is not, and does not claim to be the first composer to make true musical portraits, and it is important to examine briefly the historical precedents for Thomson's own practice. Of most importance for the purposes of this study are the four composers that Thomson cited in his 1976 article for *Antaeus*, "Of Portraits and Operas"[1] — Couperin, Schumann, Anton Rubinstein, and Elgar.

What must be the earliest significant experiments in musical portraiture date from the eighteenth century harpsichord music of François Couperin (1668-1733). In his article on Couperin which appears in the *New Grove Dictionary*, Edward Higginbottom states that the literally hundreds of character pieces and portraits of François Couperin were not unique, nor an innovation. Couperin lived in an age when "the role of music was seen as that of arousing specific feelings and thoughts in the hearts and minds of listeners."[2] A prevailing aesthetic principle in composition sought to "imitate" in music the emotions and natural phenomena of life. This expressed itself in instrumental genres by the attempt to emancipate music from dance prototypes, and by a profusion of character pieces and, ultimately, portraits. Couperin's compositions in these genres, though not unique, were notable in the force and intensity of their musical characterization.

---

[1]Virgil Thomson, "Of Portraits and Operas," *Antaeus*, 21/22 (Spring/Summer 1976), 208-210.
[2]Edward Higginbottom, "(4) François Couperin," *New Grove Dictionary of Music and Musicians* (London: Macmillan, 1980), IV, 868. (Hereafter referred to as *New Grove Dictionary*.)

The subjects of Couperin's portraits were usually friends, pupils and royal masters. His goal was to reflect the "personal qualities" of his subjects in "appropriate musical gestures." Higginbottom describes the musical portrait of Antoine Forqueray, the great viol player and a "self-assured and brilliant man," as a "proud Allemande movement with a firmly treading bass against an alert, driving treble."[3] Couperin's portraits include self-portraits, non-identified portraits, collections of contrasting personalities in dance pairs and suites, and satirical portraits. Few composers of musical portraits since Couperin—Virgil Thomson is a clear exception—have treated the genre with as much regard, as is demonstrated by the sheer volume and craft of the Couperin portraits for harpsichord.

The contributions of Robert Schumann (1810-1856) to musical portraiture, especially in his piano music, are important but more problematic. Schumann's music is strongly autobiographical and filled with literary and musical allusions. But, these allusions are often hidden, and the autobiographical content is often buried. In his interesting discussion of Schumann's piano music in the *New Grove Dictionary*, Gerald Abraham discusses the theory, held by some, that almost all themes and motives in Schumann's music derive from a "private method of musical cryptography involving correspondence between letters and notes, for example CLARA, ASCH, and ABEGG."[4] But the examples in Schumann of specific musical portraits are not frequent.

The best examples of Schumann's more explicit portraits are in *Carnival*, Op. 9. This suite of twenty-one "Scenes mignonnes sur quartre notes" is filled with musical caricatures of "comedia dell'arte" personalities, and the requisite appearances of Schumann's alter-egos, Eusebius and Florestan." But *Carnival* also contains four explicit musical portraits: "Chiarina," a passionate study in c minor of the fifteen year old Clara Wieck; "Estrella," a breathless and expansive portrait of Ernestein von Fricken (like Schumann, a piano student living in the home of their teacher and Clara's father, Frederic Wieck); "Chopin"; and "Paganini". "Estrella" and "Chiarina" are true musical depictions of the inner natures of these two young women, but "Chopin" and "Paganini" are clearly imitations of the music of these two composers.

In 1855 the Russian pianist and composer Anton Rubinstein (1829-1894) was a guest at a house-party on an island called Kamennoi-Ostrow. While there, he made twenty-three piano portraits of the various guests, and one more of the place itself. The collection was published in 1855 as *Kamennoi-Ostrow*, Op. 10, 24 Portraits for Piano.[5] This work begins to approach, at least in its conception, the compositional methods employed by Thomson in

---

[3]Ibid.
[4]Gerald Abraham, "Robert Schumann," *New Grove Dictionary*, XVI, 850.
[5]Edward Garden, "Anton Rubinstein," *New Grove Dictionary*, XVI, 299.

his own portraits. *Kamennoi-Ostrow* is the only example of explicit musical portraiture from the mid-nineteenth century of any renown.

But, prior to Thomson's portraits, the most famous set of musical portraits was by Sir Edward Elgar (1857-1934)—*The Variations on an Original Theme ("Enigma"), Op. 36.* The genesis of this work involved a series of improvisations at the piano based on a common theme but worked out in the manner or character of a dozen friends. Elgar added an improvisation based on his wife and one on himself and shaped this work into a set of fourteen variations. In her *New Grove Dictionary* article on Elgar, Diana McVeagh states that the identities of the subjects for each variation, which had been unknown, have mostly been determined. Among them are musical associates of Elgar, a country squire, and "Nimrod" (A. J. Jaegar, the publishing office manager at Novello.)[6]

The musical portraits by Elgar, Rubinstein, Schumann, and Couperin, and the methods by which they were composed represent intriguing and, to varying degrees, successful experiments in the practice of musical portraiture. But the reason there have been relatively few composers of musical portraits is simply that music is considered to be too abstract a medium for the explicit portrayal of human character and likeness.

Virgil Thomson would not contest this. A listener unacquainted with the subject of a particular Thomson portrait will listen to it solely for its intrinsic musical merit. But the musical content of Thomson's portraits is crucially determined by the fact that they are, indeed, portraits. We will see that Thomson believes that his musical portraits, in fact, "work" as portraits. But Thomson's experiments with musical portraiture were first animated by his close observation of the experiments in abstract literary portraiture by his friend and colleague Gertrude Stein. To a brief discussion of the Stein literary portraits we now turn.

[6]Diana McVeagh, "Edward Elgar," *New Grove Dictionary*, VI, 116.

CHAPTER 2

The Portraits
by Gertrude Stein

My theory was that if a text is set correctly for the sound of it, the meaning will take care of itself. And the Stein texts, for prosidizing in this way, were manna. With meanings already abstracted, or absent, or so multiplied that choice among them was impossible, there was no temptation toward tonal illustration, say, of birdie babbling by the brook or heavy heavy hangs my heart. You could make a setting for the sound and syntax only, then add, if needed, an accompaniment equally functional. I had no sooner put to music after this recipe one short Stein text than I knew I had opened a door.

— Virgil Thomson[1]

The collaboration of Virgil Thomson and Gertrude Stein is certainly one of the most fortuitous and successful artistic pairings in twentieth century arts. The abstraction of meaning in the works of Gertrude Stein gave to them—to use Thomson's phrase—a vitality based on "sound and syntax only" that was truly unique and of pivotal literary consequence in the early twentieth century. Thomson's involvement with Stein's work resulted in perhaps his most important contribution to twentieth century music: an effective and idiomatic procedure for the musical declamation of the English language. Many of the aesthetic principles and procedures of Gertrude Stein's writing were worked out in her experiments with literary portraiture. Although a detailed discussion of her portraits is beyond the scope of this book, the Stein portraits were a great impetus for Thomson's involvement with musical portraiture and some understanding of them is essential.

[1]Virgil Thomson, *Virgil Thomson* (New York: Alfred A. Knopf, Inc., 1966; New York: E. P. Dutton, Inc., 1985), p. 90.

5

In his fascinating book on Stein, *Charmed Circle,* James R. Mellow writes that the idea of literary portraits containing, in many cases, language of extreme and purposeful vagueness represents a "strange, crabbed, obstinate experiment for a writer to attempt" which "effectively consigned much of her writing to the status of closet literature."[2] Yet, despite the fact that most of these portraits were not published during her life-time, they represent an important genre of her work.

The first portrait, "Ada," from 1909, a portrait of Stein's companion Alice B. Toklas, was clearly considered by Stein to be a breakthrough in two respects. On one level, "Ada" successfully mimics the specific language style of Alice B. Toklas. The slow-moving, repetitive sentence structure of Stein's recently completed and daring work *The Making of Americans,* is replaced in "Ada" by the compact and extremely direct language of Toklas. That Stein could so masterfully mimic the language of others was an important discovery and her experiments with this technique continued. *The Autobiography of Alice B. Toklas* (1932), most notably, was Stein's rendering of the book that Alice B. Toklas could have written. In fact, in the opinion of Virgil Thomson, *The Autobiography of Alice B. Toklas* is so imitative of Toklas' language— "It's the most compact and direct writing since *Caesar's Gallic Wars,* it's pure Alice[3]—that he would not be surprised if Toklas had written some of it. Another example of this technique is Stein's *Brewsie and Willie* (1945), a rendering of the idiomatic speech and lingo of American GIs in Europe.

But the other breakthrough of "Ada" was Stein's discovery of a fresh and provocative literary genre that captured her imagination. Stein embraced literary portraiture, producing dozens of word portraits of friends, relations, and notables. Some portraits were written in pairs as in "Miss Furr and Miss Skeene" (based on Ethel Mars and Maud Hunt Squire, two painter friends of Stein), and some evolved into prolonged, book-length analyses of whole groups of people, with monotonous repetitions and extremely abstract language, for example, "Many, Many Women."

Mellow traces Stein's evolving mastery of the portrait genre and the growing economy of her language. In certain portraits, Stein continued to experiment with the mimicking of language styles. But eventually, in all portraits, Stein dispensed entirely with any narrative thread and wrote in language "purged of associative values"[4] with only hints of the subject, like word equivalents of Cubist paintings. Later on she tried short, abstract portraits of only three or four lines, like her 1912 portrait, "Guillaume Apollinaire":[5]

[2] James R. Mellow, *Charmed Circle* (New York: Avon Books, 1976), p. 168.
[3] Virgil Thomson, interview, January 18, 1985.
[4] Ibid., p. 165.
[5] Gertrude Stein, *Portraits and Prayers* (New York: Random House, 1934), p. 26.
[6] Gertrude Stein, *Writings and Lectures: 1911-1945,* ed. Patricia Meyerowitz, (London: Peter Owen, 1967), p. 108.

> Give known or pin ware.
> Fancy teeth, gas strips.
> Elbow elect, sour stout pore, pore caesar, pour state at.
> Leave eye lessons I. Leave I. Lessons. I.
>   Leave I lessons, I.

Yet Stein's intent in her portraits was quite specific. In a lecture entitled "Portraits and Repetitions," delivered in Chicago during her 1934 trip to America, Stein made quite clear her involvement with this genre:[6]

> I had to find out what it was inside any one, and by any one I mean every one
> I had to find out inside every one what was in them that was intrinsically
> exciting and I had to find out not by what they said not by what they did not
> by how much or how little they resembled any other one but I had to find it
> out by the intensity of movement that there was inside in any of them.

This quote should dispel the notion that Stein's portraits represent language derived from stream of consciousness and free association. An important influence on Stein's experiments in word portraits and, in fact, on all her writings was her study of psychology with William James as an undergraduate at Radcliffe. In the forward by Janet Flanner to the Yale edition of Stein's *Two*, the abstract "Cubist" word portraits are shown to be the product of an explicit and detailed procedure.[7] In the initial stages of her work, Stein made charts and diagrams of what she called the "bottom natures" of her subjects—both in her fiction and, especially, in her portraits—isolating the fundamentals of their characters and diagramming the resemblances of their traits to those of other people. These charts were very important to her and Stein left them with the complete collection of her manuscripts donated to the Yale Library the year before her death in 1946.

In researching the Stein portraits I sought the assistance of Donald Gallup, the curator of the Gertrude Stein Collection at the Beinecke Rare Book and Manuscript Library at Yale University. Mr. Gallup, who was a personal friend of Stein, explained that this detailed procedure of character analysis was Stein's method only with regard to the early portraits, from 1909 until about about 1915. After this period Stein wrote her portraits without preliminary written charts or drafts and, in many cases, spontaneously, in one sitting. The specifics of her procedures and the relationship of Stein's preliminary character charts to her final word portraits is not the province of this study, but it is discussed in great detail in *Exact Resemblance to Exact Resemblance: The Literary Portraiture of Gertrude Stein* (New Haven and London: Yale University Press, 1978) by Wendy Steiner.

The expressive content in many of the Stein portraits is so abstract that one is left with a virtually hermetic piece of writing. Yet, because these works

[7]Janet Flanner, "Foreword" to Gertrude Stein, *Two: Gertrude Stein and her Brother and Other Early Portraits* (Freeport, NY: Books for Libraries Press, 1969), pp. ix-xvii.

are called "portraits," the reader searches them for depictions of their subjects' characters. This has given rise to a unique type of literary scholarship, considered by many to be at odds with more traditional formal criticism. These new Stein scholars scrutinize the portraits for any traces of autobiographical data. In addition, they apply to their readings any prior knowledge they might have about the portraits' subjects.

In *Exact Resemblance to Exact Resemblance*, Wendy Steiner presents a compelling interpretation of the "Guillaume Apollinaire" portrait quoted above, an interpretation that demonstrates the effectiveness of this investigative approach to literary scholarship. Of course, to "read" this portrait one must be familiar with the formal, structural techniques of Stein's writing—for example, the disruption of word order, the permutations and repetitions of phrases, the interchange of words with their phonological equivalents—all of which are discussed in detail in Wendy Steiner's book. But only when one brings to this piece some prior knowledge of Apollinaire, especially Stein's relationship with and understanding of him, can one begin to decipher the meaning of this portrait.

For example, Wendy Steiner suggests that, on one level, the last line of the Apollinaire portrait presents various permutations on the phrase "eye lessons," a term which might be applied to Apollinaire's diagrammatic poems. The opening line, "Give known or pin ware," is a phonological echoing of the title, "Guillaume Apollinaire." Wendy Steiner's further interpretations of this portrait are quite detailed and complex, but very convincing. For example, if one knows that Gertrude Stein associated Apollinaire with his fashionable clothing and with the monocled Kaiser Wilhelm (Apollinaire was christened Wilhelm Apollinaris Albertus de Kostrowicki), and if one disrupts the word order of the first two lines of the portrait ("Give known or pin ware./Fancy teeth, gas strips."), then the reader will begin to sift out phrases like "pinstrips" (i.e., fashionable clothing), or "gas-ware" (i.e., glass ware, or the Kaiser's monocle).[8]

I am only skimming the surface of Wendy Steiner's perceptive reading of this portrait to illustrate the kind of scholarship that is currently being applied to the literary portraits by Gertrude Stein. But the relevance of this literary scholarship to the study of Thomson's musical portraits is the idea that the reader (or listener) who brings to a literary (or musical) portrait some prior knowledge of the subject will have a quite different experience of the piece from someone lacking such familiarity.

As with the musical portraits by Thomson, the Stein word portraits can also be read for their intrinsic literary merit. But to comprehend the success of a Stein portrait as a character depiction one must scrutinize them for biographical data or references. In this regard, the Stein portraits present

[8]Wendy Steiner, *Exact Resemblance to Exact Resemblance: The Literary Portraiture of Gertrude Stein* (New Haven and London: Yale University Press, 1978), p. 99.

varying degrees of challenge to the reader. Some of the word portraits are quite "readable," some are hopelessly hermetic. The 1909 portrait of Picasso, for example, is quite clear. But, in 1928 Virgil Thomson was the subject of a Stein word portrait which is an example of Stein's writing at its most abstract and obscure.

Thomson admits that even he has not been able to comprehend the specific meaning of his own portrait. In our conversations, Thomson commented:[9]

> This was done when I was in America that fall and winter for several months in 1928-29. Gertrude sent this to me saying, "You will see how much we think of you." Well, I can't tell too much about it. If you want to decipher this portrait, which I am quite unable to do, you might try Maurice Grosser [see catalog entry No. 10] because he understands me and Gertrude Stein better than I do and he may help you with it.

Having met Stein in 1926 during the period when she did not prepare charts for her portraits, Thomson knew nothing of this procedure. But with regard to this preliminary work Thomson offered the following observation:[10]

> Young writers always do more preparation than mature ones. Mature ones can get right at it and organize it while they are writing.

The manuscript of the Thomson portrait—which I examined at Beinecke Library—is written with pencil in long-hand in a lined composition booklet and contains virtually no corrections. Concerning Stein's revisions Thomson explained:[11]

> The curious thing about Stein's corrections is that when they occur they are usually things she adds. She rarely crosses out anything.

Quoted below are the first ten lines (out of a total of forty-eight) of the Virgil Thomson portrait by Gertrude Stein:[12]

> Yes ally. As ally. Yes ally yes as ally. A very easy failure takes place. Yes ally. As ally. As ally yes a very easy failure takes place. Very Good. Very easy failure takes place. Yes very easy failure takes place.
> When with a sentence of intended they were he was neighboured by a bean.
> Hour by hour counts.
> How makes a may day.
> Our comes back back comes our.
> It is with a replica of seen. That he was neighboured by a bean.

This portrait was written by Stein shortly after the completion of her first

[9]Virgil Thomson, interview held on March 16, 1982 in Brookline, Massachusetts.
[10]Ibid.
[11]Ibid.
[12]Stein, *Portraits*, p. 198.

operatic collaboration with Thomson, *Four Saints in Three Acts*, while Thomson was in the United States giving concerts and attempting to promote their new opera. The first lines appear to refer to Thomson as Stein's new "ally" and to the difficulty *Four Saints* was already having in finding an appreciative audience and sponsorship. But starting with the sentence after the first paragraph, "When with a sentence of intended they were . . . ," and especially the phrase "he was neighboured by a bean," the real obscurity begins. Following is my brief conversation with Thomson concerning this line and the interpretation of this portrait:[13]

> AT: Do you know what this line, "he was neighboured by a bean," means?
>
> VT: Well, the only thing I can think of is that I had an old friend from Kansas City who was a painter and lived in Paris and whom Gertrude knew a little bit and didn't like particularly, Eugene McCown. I've always thought that might refer to him, "he was neighboured by a bean." But you never know.
>
> AT: Did you ever sit down and ask her about this?
>
> VT: She wouldn't tell you anything. Oh no, she would never tell you anything like that. Once in a while she would gratuitously or accidentally let something out. Alice [B. Toklas] could read them. There's another piece of Gertrude's—and I don't remember what it is—in which I appear and Alice in typing the thing said, "What's Virgil doing here?" Gertrude said, "Oh, he just came in." But I don't remember what piece that was. It was something written in 1929-30 or around there.

The Thomson portrait becomes increasingly obscure and Thomson warned that one can not "just guess" at the meaning. I became increasingly determined to try to decipher this portrait with Thomson's help, so I asked him to examine it once again. Quoted in full below is the letter he wrote to me in answer:

> 20 April, 1983
>
> Dear Tony,
>
> I have never been able to make much out of my portrait by GS.
>
> Have been looking at it lately with some intensity. So has Maurice [Grosser]. Neither of us can get very far.
>
> It is quite grand, but terribly dense.
>
> Do let me know what you make of it.
>
> Everbest,
> Virgil

Apart from their intrinsic merit as works of literature, the success of Gertrude Stein's portraits as exercises in characterization certainly varies, even in the opinion of so obvious an admirer as Virgil Thomson. But Thomson was clearly impressed by the idea of depicting character through the use of language purged of its associative values so as to focus on sound and syntax.

---

[13]Thomson, interview, March 16, 1982.

In addition, and perhaps most importantly, it was the spontaneity of the creative procedure that Gertrude Stein cultivated for her portrait writing that intrigued Virgil Thomson, who in 1928 had just finished the enormous task of setting Stein's *Four Saints in Three Acts* to music and was now free to experiment. This spontaneous creative procedure might be applied to the composition of music. The implications of this idea led Thomson to begin his own experiments with musical portraiture.

Virgil Thomson and Anthony Tommasini (at piano) at Yale University —
concert "In Tribute to Virgil Thomson," April 29, 1982. (Photo by Jeff
Strong, Yale Public Information Offfice.)

CHAPTER 3

Composing a Musical Portrait: Virgil Thomson's Procedure

In 1928 Virgil Thomson wrote to Gertrude Stein: "My portrait trick is developing nicely and seems to be quite new; that is, for music, since the idea of it comes obviously out of you."[1] As we have seen, Thomson was acquainted with the musical precedents in portraiture, but only after examining Stein's abstract word portraits did he take up this genre for music. It is interesting that just as Stein's involvement with word portraits followed the completion of her important early novel *The Making of Americans*, Thomson's musical portraits followed the completion of his important first opera *Four Saints in Three Acts*. In both cases, it was only after mastering the literary and musical genres that require the greatest sophistication in the techniques of characterization (the novel and opera, respectively) that these two artists undertook their experiments in portraiture.

During the winter of 1925-26 Thomson completed his studies with Nadia Boulanger and composed what he has referred to as his " 'graduation piece' in the dissonant style of the time,"[2] the Sonata da Chiesa for E-flat clarinet, D trumpet, viola, F horn, and trombone. In the subsequent three years Thomson composed extensively, completing a significant number of mature works culminating in 1928 with *Four Saints*. His technical skills as a composer were secure. He had just produced one of the truly original works of the

---

[1]Virgil Thomson, *Virgil Thomson* (New York: E. P. Dutton, Inc., 1985), p. 123.
[2]Kathleen Hoover and John Cage, *Virgil Thomson: His Life and Music* (New York: Thomas Yoseloff, 1959), p. 134.

twentieth century, his retreat from the then current trends towards atonality and dissonance. Stein's texts had provided Thomson with opportunities to cultivate genuine compositional freedom. Stein's experiments with literary portraiture now suggested a creative method which might be applied to music to further develop his musical spontaneity.

The following excerpt, quoted at length from Thomson's autobiography, details both his enlightenment regarding what he has called the "discipline of spontaneity" and his application of it to musical portraiture:[3]

> Two years before, at Thonon on Lake Geneva, an enlightenment had come to me that made portrait writing possible. This was the very simple discovery that the classic masters, in terms of logic and syntax, did not always quite make sense. My sudden awareness of their liberties in this regard so firmly forced me to take up my own freedom that never again was I to feel that I must necessarily "know what I was doing." This meant that I could write almost automatically, cultivate the discipline of spontaneity, let it flow.
>
> Now the value of spontaneous work is often zero, especially when it merely follows reflexes, as in pianoforte improvisation. But spontaneity can be original also, if it wells up from a state of self-containment. And it was through practicing my spontaneities, at first in a primitive way, and through questioning Gertrude Stein about this method of work, which was her own, that I grew expert at tapping my resources. Making portraits of people was just beginning to serve me, as it had long served Gertrude, as an exercise not only in objectivity, but also in avoiding the premeditated. My associates at this time were many of them fine draftsman, and I had often watched them finish each drawing in one sitting. Gertrude had long before applied their way to writing. And it was from her success with this (in my view) that I was led to try it in music. My first efforts came out so well, both as likenesses and as compositions, that I was sure I had discovered something.

Thomson, who disdains the "game of influences," prefers to talk of "theft." ("There is no influence. There is only theft."[4]) Clearly, the idea that portraiture could be a context or conduit for disciplined spontaneity is Thomson's main "theft" from the portraiture practice of Gertrude Stein. Yet in my conversations with Thomson, he very explicitly stated that the Stein portraits were not "models." He said, to quote him exactly, "they simply reminded me that this could be done."[5]

This statement does not, in fact, represent Thomson's attempt to revise history. His many acknowledgements to Stein both in his writings and in our conversations specifically concerned the unique element of spontaneity with which she practiced portraiture. The Stein portraits themselves were not models, since no literary genre can actually be a specific model for a musical composition. Thomson knew of all existing precedents in musical portrai-

[3]Thomson, *Virgil Thomson*, pp. 123-4.
[4]Richard Dyer, "Virgil Thomson at 85: Celebrated and Salty" *The Boston Globe*, November 29, 1981, p. 62.
[5]Thomson, interview, March 16, 1982.

ture. But the specific kind of "stream of consciousness" creativity that Thomson observed in the works of Stein and in the work of the many important painters with whom he associated was unknown before the celebrated era of "Paris in the Twenties." He concluded that the idea of musical portraiture could be re-invented.

Gertrude Stein did not read music and did not consider herself to be very knowledgeable about music. Thomson, as I have indicated, did not know of the specific preliminary procedures involved in Stein's word portraits, did not and could not ask her about their meaning, and does not understand even his own portrait. Yet, they did discuss—eagerly and at length—the the "discipline of spontaneity," as Thomson has indicated.

Thomson "was reminded" that Stein's spontaneous method of writing could be applied to musical portraiture. This represents Stein's main "influence" on the works of Thomson and he freely acknowledges it. But their respective procedures emanated from opposite ends of a creative spectrum. Stein took the explicit medium of language, tried to purge it of its associative references and specific meanings, and attempted to create an abstract word portrait. Thomson took the abstract medium of music, tried to cultivate within it specific, referential evocative qualities, and attempted to create an explicit musical portrait. Their convergence from opposite ends of this spectrum represents their real similarity.

However, in their portraits Stein and Thomson attempted to push their respective media in directions that were unique and perhaps invalid. Therefore, they also share in common the stated acknowledgement that their portraits as exercises in character depiction may not work. Thomson told me that "the fact that my portraits turn out so differently from one another is my circumstantial evidence that they work as characterizations."[6] More than this he can not and does not claim. Thomson's remarks on the success of his portraits as portrayals of their subjects are always speculative.

However, as has been stated, the other interest for Thomson in the Stein portraits and the specific relevance of her works to the evolution of his own craft concerns the cultivation of what Thomson calls the "discipline of spontaneity." About this Thomson talks with eagerness and specificity. His remarks to me on the subject follow:[7]

> The practice of portraiture had two advantages for me. One of them is that it is an exercise in what I call the discipline of spontaneity, which is a very tough discipline. You know, let your mind alone, that's the whole problem. Of course being bound up in the university circumstance it becomes impossible. Once you get through all this damned business you've got to get rid of it. But the other advantage is that the spontaneity serves as an exercise in characterization, which you are always needing in the opera.

[6]Ibid.
[7]Thomson, interview, January 25, 1982, New York City.

This [the discipline of spontaneity] is something that college people haven't worked with. Because after all, what is a university? The center of a university is a library. A library is about the history of everything and the analysis of everything and consequently the verbalization of everything. And [students] have never really been trained so that they acquire a technique for going beyond the word. We have these techniques but they don't let you do it in college because you've got to write it out.

At the Paris Conservatory they teach improvisation in the fugal style on the general assumption that improvisation is a very strict form of composition. You can't do it without a plan. You can't just throw yourself into a subjective state and start improvising. When you come to a hole in your attention it makes a hole in the listeners attention. Actually, improvisation is practically always done in either the variation format or in the fugal texture.

Thomson's cultivation of the discipline of spontaneity, as described above, obviously affects both the form and musical content of his portraits. On one level, the attempt to portray a individual in a musical portrait provides Thomson with a spingboard for the free, yet deliberative musical "roaming" which characterizes many of these pieces. (This will be discussed more fully in Chapter V.) But the other "advantage" of portraiture is the practice it affords in musical characterization, which for Virgil Thomson—a composer of operas, ballets, documentary film music, and incidental music for the theatre—had value beyond the genre of portraits. What does characterization mean, therefore, in a Thomson portrait? What is a musical likeness?

In his article "Of Portraits and Opera," Thomson discussed the issue of musical resemblance:[8]

As to what a likeness is in music, resemblance there, like characterization in opera writing, can come from diverse directions. Music can imitate a gesture or typical way of moving, render a complexity or simplicity of feeling, evoke a style or period, recall the sound of a voice, or of birds or trumpets or hunting horns or marching armies.

In an opera or in music for film or theatre, which Thomson calls "objective music," the ability of music to imitate life is aided by visual and narrative elements. In an abstract musical portrait of a person, the specificity of this imitation is obviously weakened, especially if the aim of the portrait is to depict character or inner life. Thomson is quite explicit on this subject. Boston composer Scott Wheeler, himself the subject of a Thomson portrait, quotes Thomson as saying: "As a subject for composition, everyone's own inner life eventually becomes dull; but someone else's inner life? That's fascinating."[9]

Thomson has stated that in his portraits the physical appearance of the

[8]Virgil Thomson, "Of Portraits and Operas," *Antaeus* 21/22 (Spring/Summer, 1976), p. 208.
[9]Reported to the author by Scott Wheeler from a conversation with Thomson.

subject is not consciously depicted. Also, although Thomson has portrayed numerous painters, he never makes their art the subject of his portraits. In reference to his portraits of Picasso, "Of Bugles and Birds," Thomson wrote: "I do not try evoking visual art; in all my portraits only the sitters presence is portrayed, not his appearance or his profession."[10]

The desire to depict inner life and character in his portraits led Thomson to adapt his compositional procedure in a striking way for a musician. His first six portraits were "drawn" from memory, as Stein had done in the final stage of her work. But all the rest have been composed in the presence of the sitter. Thomson claims to be the only composer who has done portraits this way. He states that the idea for this procedure came, quite logically, from observing the numerous painters amongst whom he lived during his Paris years.

The best short account of his working method is from "Of Portraits and Operas":[11]

> There are by now a hundred or more of such portraits, all but the first six drawn from life, and each one bearing, in the judgement of persons acquainted with the sitter, some resemblance to its model. All have been sketched in silence too, usually at one sitting, save for those that comprise several sections, in which case each movement has been composed without interruption. And I do not stop to try out on the piano, to hear, correct, or criticize what I have done. Such adjustments are left for later, as is orchestral elaboration should this occur. Descriptive subtitles, such as Lullaby or Hunting Song, are also subsequent additions. My effort while at work is to write down whatever comes to me in the sitter's presence, hoping as I transcribe my experience that it will, as the painters say, "make a composition."

In conversation Thomson describes with objective, almost clinical specificity the proper positioning of his sitters. Yet this contact is clearly a personal and creative precondition for Thomson's portrait writing. The physical presence of the sitter stimulates a certain level of non-verbal, almost psychic interchange between Thomson and his subject which is clearly essential to this process. Thomson's revealing remarks about this issue are quoted at length below:[12]

> AT: When I programmed some of your new portraits recently, I had a twinge of feeling that maybe these pieces are rather personal for you.
>
> VT: Well, of course. All music is personal. Unless it's objective, as in ballet or landscape music, opera, action music, or picture music. Don't forget that in the whole history of the last 2000 years probably ninety percent of all the music is objective, either the liturgical, or vocal-explanatory, or something like that. The interior meditative music, oh, is practically eighteenth century in

[10]Thomson, *Virgil Thomson*, p. 310.
[11]Thomson, "Of Portraits and Operas," pp. 208-9.
[12]Thomson, interview, January 25, 1982.

origin. The origins of Romanticism are there. That doesn't mean that there hasn't been, before that, "double-take,"—things that proport to be objective but unconsciously are a picture of the depictor. In the same way that any photographer takes his own picture anytime he takes somebody else's picture. That's the unconscious that comes through. Photographers are particularly sensitive that way. You have to be awfully careful with newspaper photographers because their attitude towards the person they are shooting becomes a comment. They make them ridiculous, they make them glamorous.

AT: Do you ever have such attitudes?

VT: Well, I try not to be conscious about it. Of course, you can't sit in front of a person without having an attitude. If you have no contact you can't do the portrait. And if the sitter doesn't give, you can't receive. But that happened to me several times. And it was always with women of a certain age and a rather high and elaborate social position that was largely fake. There's a frame of presentation there so old and so ingrained that they can't get through it, even if they tried.

AT: Which portraits are you talking about? I wonder if I could recognize them?

VT: Well, I never could finish them, you see. I'd give up in the middle. Well, this happens with painters. If I were a painter, and if you don't give, I can't catch you.

The portrait is best made, actually, a painter's portrait is best made with a distance [distance between the painter and the sitter] of six to ten feet. The musical portrait I find to be the most comfortable about four to six. Too close, you're mixing. But at four you're separate persons. From four to six you are close enough to communicate.

AT: But I know you won't let the sitter talk at all, right?

VT: Well, you can't talk while you're writing music. Painters talk all the time with their sitters. They keep the sitter amused, keep them from going to sleep. Now, I don't mind if they go to sleep because the eye is not involved. I look a little bit to start with, but as soon as the music starts coming I practically don't look at them any more. I look at my paper. I read back from the beginning. Every time I come to an end of a breath, I read back from the beginning and attach the new on to the old. That's how you get your continuity.

AT: There are some that were done of artists while they were doing your portrait, right?

VT: I do that with painters all the time. I let them work while I work, it keeps them amused. The first one I did that way was Christian Bérard. That's the three clarinet portraits, actually. No, the first one of the three Bérard clarinet portraits. The other two I did add not from sitting. But, I knew him awfully well by that time. [See catalog entries 9, 11, and 12.]

A funny thing about the sitting is that people that you've known for years turn out to be quite unexpected when you really look at them from that point of view. And you can do people you don't know.

AT: I was just going to ask you that. You can do a portrait of someone you don't know?

VT: Oh yes, because a person you know you do as if you didn't know him.

It's in one of the writings somewhere or other[13], Picasso said when I did his portraits, "How do you do a musical portrait?" I said, "Exactly as you would do one; I put you in front of me and I look at you and I start writing." "Oh," he said, "obviously, if I work and you are in the room, everything I do is automatically your portrait."

And when I did Dora Maar, she came to my place and he came along, out of curiosity I think, and he just sat there. Obviously he got into the portrait. A very strong character. Because he couldn't be in a room without being noticed.

Thomson's insistence upon and need for contact with the personal presence of his sitters, as described above, is the most striking and unusual aspect of his procedure. He can "sketch" equally well a close friend or a stranger if he senses an ease of what is really psychic communication. If the sitter is closed and does not "give," either because of social posturing, emotional introversion, or excessive volatility of character, Thomson can not "receive" and can not compose. Thomson's sitters can sleep while being sketched because to sleep comfortably while being observed closely by someone else is a very trusting and "giving" act. But when the progress of these compositions so directly emanates from Thomson's psychic perceptions of the inner lives of his subjects, it is obviously essential for Thomson to place his sitters in a specific situation conducive both to portraiture and to this psychic exchange.

Of course, on one level, Thomson's whole procedure can be seen as the very personal method devised by one composer for facilitating his much sought-after discipline of spontaneity. Yet, Thomson describes the process of composing a musical portrait as if it were an objectively tested method with a codified set of procedures, the logical extension of which was mocked by Picasso in the story related above. Thomson believes he has found a viable "method" for writing musical portraits; though he would not urge it on another composer, he would not be displeased if it were "stolen" and put to use.

On another level, however, Thomson embraces his portraiture method as a vehicle for successful characterization. He believes that the portraits do bear some resemblances to their subjects, resemblances that those acquainted with the subjects should recognize. Yet, in the Preface to the Schirmer edition of selected piano portraits he writes that "the interest of these pieces for the musical public at large, however, must depend, of course, on whatever intrinsic merit they may be found to possess."[14]

For the intrinsic musical merit of Thomson's portraits I will make a case in the next chapter. For those listeners who find these compositions to be hopelessly abstract as portraits, Thomson accepts their lack of interest. But the

[13]See Virgil Thomson, *Virgil Thomson*, p. 310.
[14]Virgil Thomson, Preface to *Portraits for Piano Solo: Album One* (New York: Mercury Music Copr., 1948; G. Schirmer, 1969), inside cover.

musical content and structure of the portraits is crucially influenced by the unusual circumstances of their composition and by their function as character depictions. The portraits must be analyzed from that perspective.

I will end the discussion of Thomson's portraiture method with two first-hand accounts of the experience of being a subject for a Thomson portrait. The first was submitted to me by Anne-Marie Soullière, a young woman friend of Thomson who "sat" for her portrait on November 14, 1981 at Thomson's apartment in the Chelsea Hotel in New York. Thomson was very taken with this personal account and asked me for a copy of it. It reads as follows:[15]

> I sat for Virgil Thomson on November 14, 1981, the morning following the Carnegie Hall performance of *Four Saints in Three Acts*, the eighty-fifth birthday main event. We began around 11:30, both of us having been out until one the previous evening. Virgil told me that he had been up since before eight—I didn't have the same energy level.
>
> The portrait took about an hour. We sat at the dining room table, Virgil with his back to the lovely painting of the Italian rice field, me facing him and this Grosser still-life. Virgil told me to be quiet. I could read or even sleep, but I was not to talk to him while he was writing. He took a large pad of score paper, a small 3 X 5 inch plain pad for testing musical ideas, and three or four very short sharp pencils with erasers. After a few minutes, Virgil began to write. He wrote fairly constantly and seemed to change his mind about the notes very seldom. About two-thirds of the way through the piece, he got up to turn on the stove so that our lunch of Irish stew would be ready when the piece was finished. Throughout the composition process I was reading the new *Virgil Thomson Reader* and I was very quiet. When Virgil finished writing, he took the portrait and laid it on his desk, saying, "Now we put it in the refrigerator for a day." He did not want to show it to me, although I did take a peek while he was back in the kitchen with the luncheon.
>
> It was easy to see that Virgil did not want to talk about making the portrait at that time. I hope to be able to ask him what he was thinking about when I see him again. He sent the copy to me about a week later. He told me that he looks over a portrait on the day following the composing and makes any little changes he wants. Then his secretary takes care of the photo copying. My portrait arrived with a little note (attached).
>
> We celebrated the day with lunch which included along with the Irish stew, a watercress salad dressed only with olive oil and salt, a Côte Rôtie (the entire bottle), and a pear. We made coffee, ate a few Godiva raspberry cordials, and washed the dishes together. We had quite a bit of conversation about life and love, and I finally left him at four. He planned to go out to dinner with friends that evening—his energy level never fails to astound me.

The note attached to Anne-Marie Soullière's copy of her portrait read:[16]

---

[15]Anne-Marie Soullière, letter sent to author, dated January, 1982.

d. A-M
I find it a very
pretty picture and
energetic too.
See soon.
l + k
Virgil

The other account was submitted to me by Louis Rispoli, a writer and, since 1980, the personal secretary of Virgil Thomson. Rispoli's comments about Thomson's household routine and working methods are informed by his unique vantage point and charmingly recounted. His account is excerpted below:[17]

The day Virgil Thomson made my portrait, we spent a routine working morning together. That would be starting at 9:00 A.M. If that day was typical (and most of his are), he rose at 6:00, took in *The New York Times,* assembled a bit of breakfast, got back into bed with them all and had his morning. Just what he does for three hours till I get there the days I come I cannot say; no doubt he writes a bit, maybe reads from his detective novels, has sometimes a massage. One thing I'm sure about from evidence—he makes lists.

When I arrive, the bed is made, the lists reviewed, things I have "hidden" (filed away) are found, he dictates and I take down letters, I open and he reads and answers mail, we talk about and I note what might need buying at lunchtime. VT is, anybody who knows him knows, devoted to precision: he tells me exactly what he wants me to do, and I find that makes doing it all the easier. So, once I have been set up for the day, I'm mainly on my own, making calls and typing, answering the phone and the door, cooking if there's need. Virgil retires to the parlour to read or sits at his table to work. If there will be guests, he will dress, though as a rule he prefers that visitors call after lunch, mornings being precious to him. Now and then he interrupts my working if he needs something, adds items to the various lists, asks for progress reports. A little before one o'clock I call him in for signing things, we talk groceries again, and I go to lunch. This has been our basic procedure three days a week for about five years now.

It was summer (1983) when my portrait was made, afternoon and hot. I returned to the apartment I guess about 2:30, found Virgil slouched book-in-hand asleep in his favorite chair, unpacked the groceries, went to my desk and got at whatever there was left to do. Not long after, he awoke talking, and had in his face the look of a man with something urgent on his mind—I thought at the time—maybe an idea that needed writing down right away. VT came right up to me , said "How would you like to sit for your musical portrait?" He had never mentioned making a portrait of me, and expecting to be questioned about work, I did not understand right off what he was asking. When I did I wanted to yelp. Happy surprises tend to return me to the parlance of a juvenile in East Harlem, and if I had answered him spontaneously, I very probably would have said, "I could just shit with joy!". Instead, I accepted with blushing and smiling and nodding; VT went to pee.

As I waited for him to return, I worried a bit. Now that there was to be a portrait of me, I wanted that it should be the most beautiful he had ever written and that the music should portray me to advantage. I have never known anybody to say VT has been cruel or sharp in his musical characterizations, though that does not mean he has not been or could not be. I recognize in some portraits musical moments equivalent to poking fun, maybe even sometimes a bit more than that, though in almost all cases short of insult. I wanted none of that in mine (and as it turns out I got none). Also, I wished it were in my power to inspire him sufficiently to make a portrait special enough to stand out in the gallery. I'm probably not the only one among Virgil's sitters who has thought about this. Even Charles Schultz touched on this theme in the "Peanuts" cartoon strip he made about VT's portraits, where at the end of Charlie Brown's sitting before Schroeder, the page is still blank, presumably the full extent to which he stirred the composer's imagination.

In the end, I gave up these worrisome thoughts. I had no reason, I reminded myself, to doubt his favorable opinion of me as employer and friend. By the time Virgil returned, I was calm again. At the start of the sitting, I had no reserve about myself as the beheld and beheard nor of VT as the beholder and behearer.

Having on numerous occasions seen him set up for portrait-making, I knew just where I should sit, what to do and what not. I had a book that was supposed to keep me occupied, but I never really ever seriously tried to read it. Virgil got out a pad of greenish-white music paper, selected pencils, looked at me a bit (not too long, three of four seconds I would suppose), and began to write. His hand, whether he is writing words or music, is an economical one:

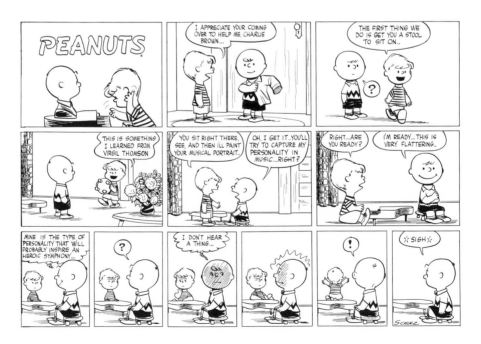

© 1954 United Feature Syndicate, Inc.

the merest pencilpoint, the thinnest-perimetered circles, attenuated lines, these on location among the staves suffice him. Eschewing everywhere the extraneous, it could not be his habit to waste time and concentration on coloring-in dots and thickening stems, nor would it be in character for him to fidget while he paused. When he is figuring something out, he looks at his paper or at his subject, sometimes hums this side of audibly, sometimes counts with his left hand, but the pencil makes no move, it seems to me, till it can with certainty, and then it does so with easy control, more like a champion gymnastic routine than a teletype. This pausing and starting goes on for a little more than an hour. When the portrait is done, VT signs it at the bottom of the page with his initials, the date, and the place.

Posing for VT, as it turned out, was much easier than sitting for a painted portrait, since all he requires is that you remain in silence and avoid interaction of any kind with him. By placing himself at a table's distance, right-angled to the sitter in profile, the subject is hardly aware of being looked at, nor is he or she able to find out anything about the portrait till it is finished. (No doubt experience convinced him there are benefits of effectiveness in these procedures; Virgil, once he has found the proper way rarely attempts another.) Since VT does not play music on the radio or stereo and does not speak, the sitter's ears are not brought to attention. Under these conditions, the sitter settles into himself or herself (most anybody has that capacity for a short time) and the artist, so disengaged from his subject, gets down to work without distraction and with a maximum of concentration.

In my case, I can't remember that Virgil ever looked up at me again, but in what seemed like a short while he announced the portrait was done, got up from the table, and left the room. I saw the music paper covered from top to bottom with lines and symbols and dots, but not reading music I made no effort to inspect it further. I must say I did feel a little bit like a father who, though by the time his child is born has long forgotten what part he may have played in producing it, feels relief and gratitude and affection toward the collaborator whose long labors are at last at an end.

These feelings were joined by a great impatience to, as Gertrude Stein said of Virgil's first setting of her words, know more than its looks. I wanted very much to carry off the manuscript right then and rush it home where I could hear it performed, but I did not ask for a dispensation from VT's "setting" rule, whereby the portrait is allowed to take on a day's character undisturbed so he can look it over with fresh eyes on the morrow for final touchups and minor adjustments. (Virgil and I try, I think, in our working together not to ask of each other questions whose answers will very probably be no.) It was not yet 5:00 P.M., but returning to desk work would have been impossible. VT suggested I leave early and I did gladly.

When Virgil signed a copy of my portrait—"For Lou my rock ever Virgil T." (secondary level of intimacy; first is "Virgil")—he said, "I think this one is quite good. And very difficult to play. Very virtuosic. It should be played quite fast." Well, late that night I reported all this to Danyal Lawson who gave me just the kind of private world premiere I wanted. He said the melodies were gorgeous and playing the portrait fast would obscure them. The music required, he said resolutely, a moderate tempo, made a case for this being more appropriate for a work written in 6/4.

I told Virgil all this the next time I saw him. He looked over the manuscript, said, "Yes, I can see that. When it is published I shall suggest both tempos."

On hearing my portrait, "Louis Rispoli: In a Boat" played for the first time, I immediately thereafter wrote and sent VT the following as a thank-you:

Virgil dear,
I love my portrait. I love you for making it so beautiful.

I should like to hear it in my pillow before sleeping. It would do as nicely as a tune for an alarm. Then what a pleasure for me coming toward and from Elysium.

I heard it for the first time it is hard to say today or yesterday when it was this side of midnight and my pianist played it for me, softly cause the neighbors do not like the piano playing late or anytime they're sleeping, and it was like a song, a mother's song, and sad for it, a little bit of sleep in it, a little lullaby to wake up with, a spinning song with daydream downbeats and no hurry in it, and that's your part I would suppose. Why we could call you gently and no rough stuff and not be half wrong and I admire that. Blessed music, no opinions in it and relief from saying yes or no there is no nonesense in it, just a poet and a mute amenuensis.

All my lifelong thanks.
Lou

Since that first performance I have heard my portrait played by more than a dozen pianists. Those who have bothered to comment praise it energetically, especially musicians familiar with the Thomson portrait canon. When Danyal gave its first public performance in Carnegie Recital Hall, Phillip Ramey ribbed me: "I didn't think you were that nice." I answered him in kind: "To Virgil, I am."

CHAPTER 4

The Portraits:
A Stylistic Survey

For composers coming of age in the early 1920s—with the profusion of radical and wildly varied compositional procedures characteristic of that era—the definition of an individual musical style often became a conscious, sometimes self-conscious intellectual decision. A streak of Kansas City independence, combined with great intellectual and cultural curiosity, led Virgil Thomson not only to a career in music and letters of astounding diversity, but to an early commitment to the free and spontaneous development of his own compositional voice. Therefore, the issue of style with regard to Thomson is elusive. It is not that he disdained an identity with a past tradition or current practice, but rather that he sought the freedom to incorporate, transform, or dismiss a current style if it obscured his own spontaneous expression.

Thomson did object, however, to the attempt to solve the dilemma of contemporary musical chaos by devotion to the strict or overly complex methods of the 1920s. The pitfalls of such devotion are evidenced for Thomson in the career of Pierre Boulez. Thomson has written that the potential of Boulez—"Europe's finest composing brain and ear" in the 1940s—has not been fulfilled because of his adherence to overly strict procedures. In a 1952 meeting Thomson told Boulez:[1]

> By using carefully thought-out and complex ways you produce by thirty a handful of unforgettable works. But by then you are the prisoner of your

[1]Virgil Thomson, *Virgil Thomson* (New York: E. P. Dutton, Inc., 1985), p. 375.

method, which is stiff. You cannot handle it with freedom, so you write less and less; at forty you are sterile. This is the trap of all style-bound artists. For without freedom no one is a master.

So Thomson has heeded his own advice and refused to throw his hat in the ring with any one "method."

Yet the specific and diverse input into Thomson's style can be clearly traced, and it is advisable for this survey to use the term "input," or "models," or anything other than "influence." Thomson on this issue is quite clear:[2]

> And as for the game of "influences" which reviewers and sometimes even historians like to play, it is in my opinion about as profitable a study as who caught cold from whom when they were all sitting in the same draft.

As a youth in Kansas City, Missouri, Thomson studied piano, organ, choir directing, accompanying, and singing from a small but first-class professional community of local musicians. By age twelve, he was himself a professional church musician and accompanist. Naturally, the melodies and sound of Baptist hymn music, in a generic and not necessarily spiritual sense, and an ingrained preoccupation with the intelligible prosody of the English language have been important elements of his style.

Despite his inbred familiarity with Baptist hymns, Thomson carefully investigated and studied Southern church music, especially "white spirituals," while working on his score for *The River*, Pare Lorentz's 1937 documentary film. Yet in some of his compositions, perhaps out of a desire to demonstrate to himself his freedom from his own musical upbringing, he has treated this hymn music with humor and, at times, even mild hostility (as in the "Variations on Sunday School Tunes" for organ, written in 1926).

While an undergraduate at Harvard, Thomson encountered three professors who exerted a decisive influence on his emerging musical personality. Archibald T. Davidson, the conductor of the Harvard Glee Club, introduced Thomson to the liturgical music of the fifteenth and sixteenth centuries. It was this modal polyphonic style, not hymn music, that was the model for many of Thomson's liturgical compositions. Professor Edward Burlingame Hill, the French-trained composer, gave Thomson his thirst for French culture and aesthetics and for French musical training. This resulted in Thomson's fifteen-year sojourn in Paris and his study with Nadia Boulanger, under whom he attained his accomplished contrapuntal technique.

Finally, Thomson was introduced to the music of Satie and the writings of Gertrude Stein by S. Foster Damon, an instructor at Harvard and Thomson's friend, though never formally his teacher. In Gertrude Stein Thomson found a kindred spirit and collaborator with whom he was to produce what

[2]Virgil Thomson, "Music Does Not Flow," *The New York Review of Books*, XXVIII:30 (December 17, 1981), p. 47

are probably his most important compositions, his operas *Four Saints in Three Acts* and *The Mother of Us All*.[3] In Eric Satie Thomson found the practitioner of a unique aesthetic creed, an alternative to the raging German complexities and the neo-classicism of the 1920s. Thomson's description of Satie's music sounds almost like an evocation of his own aesthetic philosophy:[4]

> It has eschewed the impressive, the heroic, the oratorical, everything that is aimed at moving mass audiences—it has directed its communication to the individual. It has valued in consequence, quietude, precision, acuteness of auditory observation, gentleness, sincerity and directness of statement.

In the model of Satie, Thomson seemed to find the reinforcement that he needed to follow his own instincts and to liberate himself from his academic training. The clarity, directness, diversity, and humor that is common to both composers raises the biggest "issue" with regard to Thomson's style, his simplicity.

In a revealing interview with critic John Rockwell, Thomson discussed the period in his career when he began to write more simply:[5]

> JR: Your music, whatever the degree of complexity underneath the surface, is in some rather wonderful way, I think, simple. It uses diatonic idioms, it uses short phrases, it is clear, one can hear the language in your vocal works, you pay attention to declamation. Do you think that your music's reputation in the last ten, twenty, or thirty years has suffered from a prejudice built up by the more cerebral kinds of composers?

> VT: Of course it has. It's suffered that from the time I started writing simply. Being born in 1896, I grew up as an impressionist and a neo-classical writer and in an ambiance of maximum dissonance, which was the pre-World War I set-up of Schoenberg, Stravinsky, Debussy and so forth. One hundred percent dissonant saturation, we all learned to do it. It was about 1926, when I was thirty years old that, I had a kind of enlightenment, a moment of truth if you wish, in which I said to myself, This is old-fashioned and there is very little profit to be derived from trying to continue it beyond its present masters. What I had better do is write as things come into my head rather than with any preoccupation of making it stylish and up-to-date, and it was the discipline of spontaneity, which I had come into contact with through reading Gertrude Stein, that made my music simple.

Thomson further states that he maintained at least this basic simplicity even in his numerous compositions since the 1920s that have "complex setups;" he reinforces the idea that this simplicity was an aesthetic goal arrived at by an "elaborate education." Thomson argues that to see Satie's compositional creed as a kind of deliberate naivety is a great misunderstanding. Satie, he

[3]Richard Jackson, "Virgil Thomson," *New Grove Dictionary*, XVIII, p. 786.
[4]Ibid., p. 788.
[5]John Rockwell, "A Conversation with Virgil Thomson," *The Virgil Thomson Reader* (Boston: Houghton Mifflin, 1981, p. 527

states: "...was not either *simpliste* or *simpliciste*; he was a man looking for clarity rather than for resemblances to other people."[6]

The prejudice towards excessive complexity, at least among the intellectual-academic elite, remains. The simplicity of Thomson's music promotes clarity, directness of expression, even audibility. The "personal element" in his music, as described by Peggy Glanville-Hicks in her article on Thomson for *The Musical Quarterly*, lies:[7]

> ...where it most belongs—in the emotional content, the organic whole of the music rather than in its terms of expression. It is at the source that his expression is original.

The simplicity of expression in Thomson's style is also related to one of the two movements with which he has in any way been associated, the aesthetics and creed of Dada. In the proponents of the Dada movement Thomson found a sympathetic band of creative artists whose ideological beliefs coincided with his own emerging need to liberate himself.

The main tenets of Dadaism are discussed in relationship to Thomson's work in the excellent Glanville-Hicks article. She cautions that great misunderstanding exists concerning Dada and describes the foundation of its creed as:[8]

> ...a process for debunking old forms, stuffiness, pomposity and sham, of revalidating art's components from their entombment in banal formulas, of extricating symbols from old concepts for a reassemblage in new vivacious fantasies and arrangements.

The iconoclasm of this creed fascinated Thomson. His emerging technical mastery of diverse styles and musical forms coincided with the ideological tenets of Dadaism, where the use by free impulse in a collage-like manner of totally incongruous elements suggested, to quote Thomson biographer Kathleen Hoover, "a new and vital mode of extending music's vocabulary, a way of saying fresh things by fresh means."[9] Styles and moods, even themes could be lifted from one context, from one era and transposed to another. The form and idiom of different contexts could be merged.

The earliest explicit example of this idiomatic mixing in Thomson's music is the *Symphony on a Hymn Tune* from 1928, where the materials that generate a well-structured, "neo-classical" symphony are Baptist hymn tunes. But the portraits, especially, are filled with collage-like juxtapositions of idioms and styles; "wrong-note" modal counterpoint, "out of focus" hymns, dances, and diverse character pieces abound in the portraits.

The other artistic movement with relevance to Thomson, and the only

[6]Ibid., p. 528.

[7]P. Glanville-Hicks, "Virgil Thomson," *The Musical Quarterly*, XXXV (19490, p. 209.

[8]Glanville-Hicks, "Virgil Thomson," p. 210.

[9]Kathleen Hoover and John Cage, *Virgil Thomson: His Life and Music* (New York: Thomson Yoseloff, 1959), p. 51.

movement with which he has specifically linked himself, was the "Neo-Romanticism" of the early 1930s led by the painter Christian Bérard. In an era where the most important activity in music consisted of the evocation of music's past in the new languages codified in the 1920s, Thomson wrote in his 1966 autobiography that the novelty of the neo-romantics, "and I am speaking of less than a dozen poets, painters and musicians, consisted in the use of our personal sentiments as subject matter."[10]

The simple tenet of this movement was that painting and music were in danger of becoming evocative arts and, therefore, the depth and seriousness of personal expression would reassert itself as legitimate subject matter for art. However, in his 1977 interview with John Rockwell, Thomson greatly qualifies the importance of this movement to his own work. He considers himself to be, by nature, a very "unromantic character" and consigns this movement more properly to painting.[11]

The particular character of Thomson's stylistic variety will be clarified more specifically in the subsequent analyses of individual Thomson portraits. But it is important to understand that Thomson, without any preconceived bias, has adopted throughout his career any useful stylistic or technical means of composition from any source. As John Cage has written:[12]

> Virgil Thomson can be seen to be as unbiased as he is active in his quest for useful means. Dedicated to no technique, he continually observes his surroundings; and when his eye lights on something he deems of use to his purposes, nothing in him restrains his taking it. Even his purposes move about, sometimes toward the expression of his sentiments, sometimes to the acceptable-to-him expression of everyone's sentiments. The opportunity offered and made sufficiently attractive, he will leave neo-romanticism, social realism, or any other "ism" and energetically take up abstraction, Dada, or whatever. But he is never aimless.

The musical styles of the 140 musical portraits by Virgil Thomson vary, obviously, with the specific personalities being portrayed. Yet the vast majority of the portraits were composed in groups, prompted in several instances, by Thomson's completion of a major set of works and his resulting need to exercise again the "discipline of spontaneity." This was confirmed by Thomson in conversation:[13]

> AT: In the first portraits for solo violin, written right after *Four Saints*, the musical language is totally different from that of *Four Saints*. Don't you think so?
>
> VT: Well, the next thing always is. You know, you don't repeat what you've just done.

[10]Thomson, *Virgil Thomson*, p. 156.
[11]Rockwell, *Virgil Thomson Reader*, . p. 526.
[12]Hoover/Cage, *Virgil Thomson*, p. 184.
[13]Thomson, interview, January 25, 1982.

AT: It seems as if you were almost looking for some way in which to let off some steam.

VT: Well, one always is.

Clearly, Thomson turned to the portrait genre as a special outlet for his evolving compositional preoccupations. Despite the fact the portraits were intended to mimic the unique and different personalities of their subjects, they were frequently produced in groups with definite stylistic similarities, often reflecting a stylistic departure from Thomson's previous compositional preoccupations.

The remainder of this chapter will survey the portraits as an entire genre of compositions and discuss the specific impetuses for Thomson's periodic pre-occupation with portrait writing. In the subsequent chapter, stylistic charac-teristics and formal organization plans—concepts introduced in this survey—will be analyzed with respect to four representative piano portraits. With regard to their harmonic vocabulary, the various groups of portraits evidence Thomson's experiments in many diverse idioms including: chromaticism, atonality, bitonality, polyharmony, straight-forward and tuneful diatonic harmony, and the distinctive language that resulted from Thomson's appli-cation of the laws of counterpoint to lines of dissonant intervals.

With regard to their formal organizational schemes, the portraits share one characteristic of primary importance—a very deliberate quality of linear continuity. This characteristic is of course present in the many Thomson portraits written in traditional polyphonic forms—canons, fugues, and strict two and three line pieces. But even the portraits that are dance forms, char-acter pieces, and tonal sectional forms (da capo ABA forms, three-movement sonatas) possess a strong quality of continuity. Even the many pieces that are "collage-like" juxtapositions of athematic material project a remarkable sense of continuity.

It will be remembered that in the interview quoted in Chapter III, Thom-son described the process by which he constantly reads back from the begin-ning while composing a portrait and attaches the "new" onto the "old." ("That's how you get your continuity."[14]) Thomson further elaborated upon his procedure for achieving continuity in his music, especially his portraits, during an interview part of which is quoted below:[15]

> Any music has to have continuity. If your continuity is a thematic or har-monic structure in an eighteenth-century vein, then you can do anything you want to on top of it. But if it's the modern non-repetitive system, you have to make a kind of occult continuity by psychological means. That's why when I'm doing these [portraits] in front of somebody, every time I come to a breath in a phrase I read back from the beginning and attach the next one on to that

[14]Thomson, interview, January 25, 1984.
[15]Thomson, interview, March 16, 1982.

so the whole thing will have a kind of curve. But, that is almost never thematic. Sometimes it's a kind of motivic unity and sometimes it's a jerky continuity. It isn't put together statically. It's more like film cutting except that it is not done with already existing material. But in film cutting no two shots are alike. You make one follow the other to tell the story or give the situation.

There are other technical things involved [in film editing] such as when the light goes out of any character's eyes, you end that section. If I'm writing and I come to the end of a phrase, or a period, or something that has said what it has to say, but the piece isn't finished, I do the thing that I think of next and attach it right on. But I read back from the beginning to see if it does attach. That's all I can really tell you about the matter.

A strong sense of linear, almost narrative continuity permeates all the compositions of Thomson. This was the very element Thomson so admired in the Stein librettos—a perfect sense of continuity achieved by Stein's mastery of repetitive structure. Thomson set *Four Saints* to music (all of the text, even the stage directions!) without any alterations to the repetitive continuity and successful structure of the text. Another technique for achieving continuity discussed often by Thomson is the purposeful avoidance of climaxes. In an interview with Kevin Miller in 1981 on WERS-FM radio station in Boston, Thomson remarked that the avoidance of climax in the music of "the repetitive boys, you know, Glass and Reich," was "rather entertaining." He then further stated:[16]

> If you avoid climactic formulas, you can make a piece go on for days. But if you start making a climax, then you have a beginning, a middle, and an end.

Even with respect to performance practice, especially in vocal music, Thomson above all else insists on a strong sense of linear continuity. During one discussion with him, Thomson made the following comments about bad performance habits:[17]

> My *bête noir*, of course, is what I call "hairpins." Constant diminuendo and crescendo and a ghastly habit of ending every phrase as if it were a feminine ending. I mean they chop the piece into little sections like that. [Chops air with hand.] The very grand and experienced performers know better than that. And the opera singers. Mary Garden especially.

And on the subject of the Mozart piano sonatas:

> Never, never, never make a feminine ending in Mozart. [Thomson stands up and sweeps his arm above his head.] Keep it in the air! Keep it in the air!

These statements by Thomson reinforce his particular concern with the element of continuity in his music, especially the portraits. Thomson's portraits are the products of his musical ruminations on the inner natures of his

[16]Thomson, interview, WERS-FM radio station, Boston, February 26, 1981.
[17]Thomson, interview, January 25, 1982.

sitters, sketched during sitting sessions that rarely last for more than one and one-half hours. This procedure results in compositions that are all relatively short and that project a kind of discursive, linear continuity despite the variety of their organizational and harmonic schemes.

A great many of the portraits are relatively straight-forward contrapuntal pieces—free two and three part compositions, canons, fugues, and inventions. About the use of contrapuntal music for character depiction in his portraits Thomson explained that "people with strongly organized characters very often turn out to be canons or fugatos or something like that." Polyphonic pieces possess an intrinsic quality of linear continuity and a "sort of inborn organization."[18]

One final issue of general importance which must be discussed before a general survey of the Thomson portraits is begun is Thomson's employment of titles. Most of the Thomson portraits have some kind of musically descriptive title and are simply subtitled "A Portrait of (Subject)." Thomson explained quite clearly the procedure by which he selects a title and its importance in one conversation:[19]

> There is no system. It's just whatever I can think of. I think it's nice if they can have a musical title as well as an identity. You see, I don't write these titles until a long time afterwards. I find what is in the piece and see what I can do about it. But I think these pieces ought to have some title, either an invented one or a musical one like Waltz or Polonaise or something other than mere identification which means nothing to people not acquainted with the subject.

One good example of this practice relates to the portrait of Henry McBride—the art critic for the *New York Evening Sun* during the 1930s—which is entitled "Tennis"(27).[20] McBride was clearly one of those subjects with a "strongly organized character," as Thomson put it. McBride inspired a contrapuntal portrait with bitonal, clashing canonic elements. Afterwards, Thomson realized that this was an appropriate musical expression of not only McBride's character but his passion for the game of tennis. After composing this portrait, Thomson realized that he had "made a tennis game—oh yes, you bat that ball forward and smash it and do all the tennis things in there."[21]

Any survey of the entire body of Thomson portraits must refer extensively to the only-book length study of Thomson, *Virgil Thomson: His Life and Music* by Kathleen Hoover and John Cage. The book is divided into Hoover's discussion of Thomson's life (which is brief and predates even Thomson's 1966 autobiography) and Cage's discussion of Thomson's music.

---

[18]Thomson, interview, March 16, 1982.
[19]Ibid.
[20]All numbers in parentheses refer to each portrait's individual numbering in the thematic catalog (see Appendix).
[21]Thomson, interview, March 16, 1982.

Thomson explained his relationship to the Hoover/Cage study and his opinion of it in our conversations:[22]

> [The Hoover/Cage] book is a splendid bibliography. And for analytical purposes Cage inspected and described every single fragment of my manuscripts in existence at the time, which ended in 1959. And for publication purposes I went over it with him because Mrs. Hoover thought it needed a little editing and I said I would do it, but not tampering with opinions. So I did check the analyses with him and occasional bits of phraseology. But I very strictly didn't attempt to alter or modify any of his judgments or expressions of opinion. His method of rhythmic analysis is far in advance still of what is taught in the colleges. The colleges don't do rhythmic analysis to my knowledge. He and Lou Harrison and probably Hovhaness know all about that. Cage was not so expert at harmonic analysis as he was at rhythmic analysis. But he was very good at knowing what a piece was about and was good at describing pieces.

Cage does penetrate many of the more iconoclastic aspects of some of Thomson's music. His descriptions are often colorful and apt. (I will quote from them often.) But some of Cage's analyses tell as much about him as they do about Thomson, filled as they are, for example, with statistics about how many C's occur in a particular piece. The rhythmic analysis is insightful and the advocacy of Thomson's music genuine. But many of the Cage analyses are idiosyncratic to a fault.

* * *

The very first portrait was written by Thomson on July 21, 1928 while he was staying in the Basque lands in France shortly after completing the composition of *Four Saints in Three Acts* (the piano-vocal score, the orchestration was not completed until 1933). A young Spanish woman who played the violin had asked Thomson to write something for her. In his autobiography, Thomson describes his inspiration for this portrait:[23]

> She had a way of entering the hotel's dining arbor with assurance, her equally self-assured mother one step behind, that pleased me because this granting of priority to youth, in Europe uniquely Spanish, was also our American way. Otherwise, the mother and daughter were not of American pattern; they were almost like sisters, happy together, discussing but not chattering, alert in repose, occupying themselves while waiting for the evening, and not surprised that a particular evening would bring no mating male, though when it did they would be ready, for Spain is a timeless image of eternity. All this plus some gesture (Spanish gesture) I endeavored to depict in music; and although the piece was written to be played without piano, I called it a *Portrait of Señorita Juanita de Medina Accompanied by Her Mother.* As a matter of fact, the mother later asked permission to compose an accompaniment for it, and did.

Señorita de Medina (1) was followed by six more portraits for solo violin all

---

[22]Ibid.
[23]Thomson, *Virgil Thomson*, p. 123.

completed between July and November of 1928: *Madame Marthe-Marthine* (2), *Georges Hugnet, Poet and Man of Letters* (3), *Cliquet-Pleyel in F* (4), *Miss Gertrude Stein as a Young Girl* (5), *Mrs. C.W.L.* (6), *Sauguet* (7). The first six portraits were composed from memory, but starting with Sauguet's portrait, all subsequent Thomson portraits with a very few exceptions have been composed in the presence of the sitter, or, as Thomson states in the Sauguet manuscript, "d'après nature."

The style of the first two solo violin portraits represents an experiment in advanced chromaticism approaching atonality. In his discussion of these portraits in *Virgil Thomson: His Life and Music*, John Cage points out that all twelve tones appear four times (with the exception of C sharp and F sharp the last time) in the compositions sixty measures, and in *Madame Marthe-Marthine* all twelve tones appear five times (again with the exception of F sharp the last time) in fifty-nine measures. The second phrase of *Marthe-Marthine*, mm. 8-11, containing all twelve tones is quoted below (Figure 1):

Figure 1.

Thomson's adoption of this excessively chromatic harmonic language resulted from the convergence of two distinct motivations. Thomson had just completed the most large-scaled and important work of his career to date, *Four Saints in Three Acts*, written in a distinctive tonal idiom with simple harmonies and clear textures. He was now looking for an outlet in which to reactivate his imagination and turned not only to the genre of the portrait, but to a fresh chromatic language.

The other motivation for this new vocabulary was more oblique. Thomson was interested in exploring the more idiomatic and specialized capabilities of stringed instruments. Glanville-Hicks points out in her article on Thomson that having mastered orchestral string writing, Thomson was now interested in exploring the technical resources peculiar to virtuoso string writing, often associated with the bravura nineteenth-century violin repertoire. Consequently, the violin portraits contain implicit allusions both to nineteenth-century virtuoso string technique and to the chromatic harmonic language common to that era.[24]

The next two portraits return to relatively straight-forward diatonic tonality. *Gertrude Stein* is entirely in B-flat, and *Cliquet-Pleyel* is in F, although it

[24]Glanville-Hicks, "Virgil Thomson," p. 220.

contains passages of an atonal character that Cage describes as being "so placed as to give a feeling of flying off the handle."[25] The portraits *Hugnet* and *Sauguet* are very atonal, and *Mrs. C.W.L.*, though beginning in E-flat, is "engulfed," to use Cage's term, by atonality at its conclusion.[26]

In December of 1928, while on a trip to the United States to perform his own works and promote *Four Saints*, Thomson received a commission from the first clarinettist of the Boston Symphony, Gaston Hamelin, for a composition scored for clarinet ensemble. Thomson complied with *Five Portraits for Four Clarinets*, written during June and July of 1929. These pieces—scored for clarinets in B-flat and A, basset horn (later rescored for the more available clarinet in E-flat), and bass clarinet—use the same palette of tonal and atonal harmony, but incorporate musical materials new to the portraits: witty "wrong note" diatonicism, canonic writing, and a striking passage—in the *Portrait of Ladies*—of superimposed scales which travel at different speeds to a downbeat climax. Cage also suggests that these pieces advance the formal element of athematic, non-repetitive continuity that was to become a central feature in many of the subsequent Thomson portraits.[27]

During the next seven months Thomson wrote some songs on French texts and his first two piano sonatas. The Piano Sonata No. 1 was later orchestrated as Thomson's Symphony No. 2 in 1931; the Piano Sonata No. 2 (along with a portrait from 1956, *Homage to Marya Freund*) was incorporated in *Autumn*: the Concertino for Harp, Strings, and Percussion—a nine minute piece from 1964 commissioned by the Northern California Harpists Association for Nicanor Zabaleta. But the Piano Sonata No. 2, according to Thomson, is also a portrait, in fact, as he put it, perhaps "the portrait of them all!" Thomson considers this piece to be a self-portrait, a "Portrait of the Artist as a Young Man," a work that is "intensely about my own inner life of that time."[28]

Thomson explains that although this sonata is not overtly a portrait, he "suspects" it of being a musical self-portrait which, as opposed to a self-portrait by a painter, is a hard thing for a composer to recognize. But he did not realize this himself until he transformed the sonata into the Concertino. Thomson wanted to call the piece "Portrait of An Artist as a Young Man," but the harpist Zabaleta objected and Thomson did not insist.

The Piano Sonata No. 2 is not formally a portrait and is not listed in the thematic catalog. But the characteristics of this piece that have led Thomson to the "suspicion" that it is a self-portrait are revealing and are quoted below:[29]

[25]Cage, *Virgil Thomson*, p. 160.
[26]Ibid.
[27]Cage, *Virgil Thomson*, p. 160.
[28]Thomson, interview, New York, August 27, 1984.
[29]Thomson, interview, New York, August 27, 1984.

AT: Isn't, in a sense, every composition a portrait of yourself?

VT: No, no. no! The Violin Sonata [from 1930] is a portrait of a young man in love. I learned that later when I had to explain it to a violinist. It's a kind of intense self-portrait. The Piano Sonata No. 1, which is the original of the Second Symphony and which works perfectly well in both cases, that's not a self-portrait. [The Piano Sonata No. 1] presents a dramatic situation which moves forward. But of course in plain instrumental music the author is always in it. To some degree it's always about of one's private life.

AT: But does the Second Sonata have a kind of quality that seems to you especially revealing or vulnerable?

VT: Well, I very slowly learned that it isn't anybody else, you see. So it has to be me. I couldn't figure out for the longest time why this piece I was so devoted to wasn't easily understood. The First Sonata is very easily understood, because it's a shape, it's self-contained, like an egg.

AT: The Second Sonata is curious.

VT: And it's very intensely me. Not me thinking about myself, but me being myself. That's why I couldn't identify it for thirty years.

On one level, the qualities of the Piano Sonata No. 2 that compelled Thomson to regard it as a self-portrait—as opposed to any other of his instrumental pieces—are elusive. That the sonata is in fact a self-portrait is Thomson's personal "suspicion." But if his comments regarding the first two piano sonatas are examined closely, it appears that the significant distinction between them relates, once again, to the important issue of formal, structural continuity. The Piano Sonata No. 1 has an almost narrative (a "dramatic situation") structural logic—it's "self-contained, like and egg."

The Piano Sonata No. 2, on the other hand, presents no such logical plan. It is discursive and volatile—dramatic but not a "dramatic situation." It lacks a sense of internal, structural logic and has not been, in Thomson's opinion, "easily understood." It is engaging music and its emotional resonance is compelling, but "its shape" is not a formal musical one, based as it is on something inherently illogical, a complex personality—Thomson's own. But, all of Thomson's pronouncements on the Piano Sonata No. 2 are "speculative." This work is not overtly a portrait and is therefore not listed in the thematic catalog.

During this busy seven-month period in 1929, Thomson also wrote ten portraits, the first seven scored for piano solo, and three more for violin and piano. This new genre had clearly captured Thomson's imagination, for these piano portraits evidence a great diversity of stylistic and formal thinking. Cage describes *Alice Branlière: Travelling in Spain (13)* as being full of "deliberate non-sequitur."[30] Although basically atonal, this portrait contains completely unexpected phrases comprised of scale passages and waltz fragments. *Alice Branlière* presents the first example of what Cage describes as

[30]Ibid., p. 163.

Thomson's "outrageously dull endings" in the portraits.[31] The last seven measures of this piece are quoted below (Figure 2):

Figure 2.

These uninteresting endings become noticeable in many subsequent Thomson portraits. However, Cage never discusses what seems to me to be the obvious reason for the use of such endings. If, as I have suggested, many of Thomson's portraits represent his musical ruminations on the nature of the sitter as captured in a short athematic composition where continuity is sought at the expense of climax, then a climactic or dramatic ending becomes not only unnecessary but potentially problematic. The music of the portraits reflects not only the character of the sitter, but Thomson's involvement with the actual experience of composing the portraits. During our discussions Thomson explained that, on one level, the endings of the portraits are reflections of a particular sitting session's conclusion. When the session is ending, after an hour or so, he explained that:[32]

> ...you don't just stop. You bring it [the portrait] to an end, and if that end seems to drag itself out you write it down. The endings are longer than they should be for so short a piece. Well, that's the way they come out. But it's not systematic.

Alice Branlière was followed by *Alternations (14)*, the Maurice Grosser portrait, which—though harmonically conservative in relationship to its predecessor—retains a quality of athematic continuity that will be analyzed in more detail in Chapter V. The next portrait, *Catalan Waltz (15)*, based on Ramon Senabre, is one of the first examples of the dance portraits—portraits that evoke dance idioms in rhythm, texture, and formal structure. In this case, the dance character is undermined by "wrong-note" harmony, athematic elements, and, to use Cage's phrase, "collage-like juxtapositions."[33] Cage also points out that three of the portraits in this group—*Clair Leonard's*

[31]Ibid.
[32]Thomson, interview, March 16, 1982.
[33]Cage, *Virgil Thomson*, p. 163.

Profile (16), *Madame Dubost chez elle (17)*, and *Jean Ozenne: Pastorale (18)*—all end by continuing the musical movement above and below a sustained pedal tone, and then prolonging the pedal tone until the conclusion of the piece.[34]

The next three portraits from 1930—*Alice Toklas (19)*, *Mary Reynolds (20)*, *Anne Miracle (21)*—are scored for violin and piano, the first three of a total of six that Thomson has written for violin and piano. In 1940 Thomson wrote another portrait for this duo, *Yvonne de Casa Fuerte (47)*, but did not turn to this scoring again until 1983 with *Cynthia Kemper (118)*, and *Lili Hastings (128)*.

There are two anecdotes regarding these attractive violin and piano portraits. First, all six are portraits of rather elegant, educated, and charming women. In fact, five of them have recently been published by G. Schirmer under the group title *Five Ladies*. (*Lili Hastings* had not been composed when the plans for this edition were finalized.) I asked Thomson about the coincidence of the violin and piano portraits all being depictions of rather elegant women. In conversation, Virgil Thomson can deliver even brief and rather cryptic observations with such sweeping certainly that no objection seems possible. One such characteristic statement follows:[35]

> I don't know. Those violin and piano portraits, it turns out, they're all women. And maybe women work better in the two dimensions.

The other anecdote regarding these violin and piano portraits concerns their release for performance. In conjunction with this study I was concerned that Thomson examine any portraits that had been left in sketch form and determine whether they might be suitable (after revision, if needed) for release. The first four violin and piano portraits—*Alice Toklas*, *Mary Reynolds*, *Anne Miracle*, all from 1930, and *Yvonne de Casa Fuerte* from 1940—were all sketched by Thomson from sittings and then, more or less, shelved; they were never performed. I was particularly eager to have Thomson release any portraits scored for violin and piano, an instrumental combination for which he writes extremely effectively. (The Violin and Piano Sonata from 1930 is a handsome, lyrical, sure-fire crowd-pleaser that is too seldom programmed.) Thomson agreed to reexamine these portraits.

To his surprise, Thomson discovered that these portraits were quite presentable and quite effective. With but minor revisions they were ready for performance. On 22 November, 1982 Thomson wrote to me: "I am overjoyed that you like these pieces. So do I, and I can't imagine why I had never done anything about them." I presented the first performance of these portraits at Wesleyan University in 1983 with violinist Sharan Leventhal.

Herein is a lesson for young artists: whether a work is "finished" or not is a debatable issue, subject to time, perspective, and one's particular mood on a particular day. Upon reexamining these early portraits (in this case, pieces written fifty years earlier), Thomson was not even able to remember what

[34]Ibid., p. 165.
[35]Interview, New York, June 20, 1984.

the problems were that led him to set them aside in the first place. He simply treated these portraits as if they were the works of another composer, in need of a little editing.

This first large group of portraits—twenty-two total, written during 1929-30—was completed by *Russell Hitchcock, Reading (22)*, a piece that combines vertical, harmonic wedges of parallel sixths with a fanciful and unexpected outburst as an ending. This was to be Thomson's last portrait for five years.

During the years from 1932 to 1934, Thomson, living again in the United States, was preoccupied with orchestrating, casting, and rehearsing *Four Saints* for its premiere at the Wadsworth Athenaeum in Hartford on February 8, 1934. For a period of twenty months he composed no new music. In late 1934 and the first months of 1935 Thomson wrote his String Quartet No. 2, and a Mass for Two-Part Chorus. Then, in April and May of 1935 Thomson composed ten portraits for piano, all in New York City.

Therefore, the impetus for Thomson's return to the portrait genre seems again to have been his completion of an intense period of work. In this new group of portraits Thomson gave nourishment to his sense of spontaneity and produced pieces of great diversity and fancy.

Although this group contains some portraits that are relatively straightforward character pieces—for example, *A. Everett Austin: The Hunt (30)* and *Josiah Marvel: Hymn (31)*—others have stylistic elements that are striking, even provocative. As in some earlier portraits, these too contain dissimilar sections of music, juxtaposed in a collage-like manner. But, the sections are extended in length, calling greater attention to the dissimilarities, and making the juxtapositions, in Cage's phrase, "more unequivocal."[36] One example, *R. Kirk Askew, Jr. (24)*, begins with an opening section of ambiguous tertial harmony, followed by a middle section of harmonically static three-part counterpoint, concluded by an atmospheric evocation of the opening melody over a bass which alternates the tritone F-B for fourteen (!) measures.

But a striking and new stylistic characteristic in this portrait group is their bitonal harmonic language. Thomson employed bitonality of a type that at times produces austere and extremely dissonant harmony. Two examples from the portrait *Paul Bowles: Souvenir (29)* well illustrate this point. In mm. 9-10, G-flat major is combined with a whole-tone passage in thirds from B-flat to F-sharp (Figure 3):

Figure 3.

m. 9   10

[36]Ibid., p. 175.

A passage from mm. 20-21 combines A-minor with C-sharp major (Figure 4):

Figure 4.

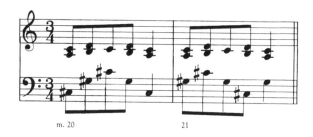

Another portrait from this group, *Henry McBride: Tennis (27)*, contains extremely dissonant bitonal canonic figurations juxtaposing the keys of C-major and D-major.

Thomson has written revealingly about the issue of bitonality and polyharmony (which implies a more momentary harmonic complex of juxtaposed chords). In his recent article for *The New York Review of Books* entitled "Music Does Not Flow"—adapted from a James Lecture delivered at New York University in 1981—Thomson wrote:[37]

> Real chords sounded simultaneously can, of course, create a polychordal complex, and the acoustic principles that govern the use of these in composition, as well as the psychological ones involved in their perception, merit investigation by composers as well as psychologists. Polyharmony is after all a natural extension of the contrapuntal principle.

Thomson suggests that polyharmony should be perceived not just as tonal dissonance but as a horizontal simultaneity of independent chordal lines. To do so, we must adjust our nineteenth- and twentieth-century predilection for perceiving music vertically to a more linear awareness, as is essential when listening to complex contrapuntal music from the medieval period. The difference, of course, is that in a polyharmonic idiom the layering involves not only single lines, but intervals and whole chords. That the tonalities involved may be dissimilar should not interfere with the perception of polyharmonic music as primarily linear. In fact, conflict between key areas can highlight contrapuntal independence of line.

There are several good examples of this technique in Thomson's subsequent group of five piano portraits written in September of 1935, bringing the total for that year to fourteen. While on vacation in Maine Thomson wrote *Miss Agnes Rindge: Prelude and Fugue (33)*, *Helen Austin at Home and*

---

[37]Virgil Thomson, "Music Does Not Flow," *The New York Review of Books*, XXVIII:30 (December 17, 1981) p. 48.

Abroad (34), and *Jere Abbott: Meditation* (35). Later in the month, while visiting two friends in Connecticut, Thomson wrote *Harold Lewis Cook: Connecticut Waltz* (36) and *Herbert Whiting: A Day Dream* (37).

Helen Austin at Home and Abroad is a particularly good example of the superimposition of parallel intervals described above. The piece begins in two-part counterpoint but evolves into a succession of passages featuring fourths against single notes, thirds against thirds, fourths against fourths, seconds against fourths and finally, to borrow Cage's phrase, fourths "waltzed against fourths" until the end.[38] More pervasive than the polyharmonic dissonance in this portrait is the clearly projected contrapuntal texture of superimposed intervals, as is shown in the following short excerpt from mm. 35-38 (Figure 5):

Figure 5.

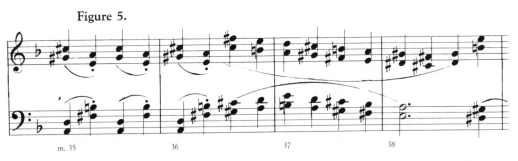

Jere Abbott is another good example of this practice, a technique that will remain important to Thomson and is used frequently in his most recent portraits.

In 1936 Thomson wrote his important film score for the Pare Lorentz documentary *The Plough That Broke the Plains*, and numerous smaller works. The following year he received a number of commissions from the Works Progress Administration (WPA) — the Depression era federal employment program. Under the auspices of the WPA Thomson wrote incidental music for numerous theatrical productions and his celebrated film score for another Lorentz documentary, *The River*.[39] In addition, during 1937 Thomson composed his ballet *Filling Station* for Lincoln Kirstein's Ballet Caravan. This period of intensive work was followed by a decision in 1938 to return to Paris and to return, not surprisingly, to the composition of portraits.

In mid-August, during a well-deserved vacation at a resort in Lamoura in southern France, Thomson "relaxed" by writing three portraits in three days, two of them scored for piano "white-notes only"—*Claude Biais* (38) and *A French Boy of Ten: Louis Lange* (39). The third, *Maurice Bavoux* (40), remained in sketch form until Thomson recently edited it for addition to the

---

[38]Ibid., p. 176.
[39]In 1949 Thomson received the only Pulitzer Prize in music ever awarded to a film score for his music to Robert Flaherty's *Louisiana Story*.

volume of piano portraits published by Boosey & Hawkes in 1981. For these three portraits Thomson's subjects were young French boys staying at this resort in Lamoura, none of whom knew Thomson at the time, all of whom agreed to sit for him.

Thomson's intention to resume again his career in Paris was interrupted by the increasing menace of World War II. The confusion of events and uncertainty about the wisdom of remaining in Paris led Thomson to turn almost exclusively to the portrait genre for his compositional sustenance. As his resolve to leave firmed, Thomson put aside all thought of large-scaled projects and wrote, between April 1 and July 9 of 1940, twenty-five piano portraits.

The intensity of Thomson's preoccupation with portrait writing reflects another aspect of his personal circumstances during the spring of 1940. Except for extended visits to the United States in the 1930s, Thomson had lived in Paris since 1925. The cataclysm of World War II had already begun. Thomson could not be certain that he would ever see again his many European friends and colleagues. He visited among them, making portraits as if he were taking photographs. These twenty-five piano portraits are, in effect, Thomson's musical photograph album of that experience. Although, in fact, Thomson returned to Paris frequently after the war, he was not to write another portrait there until 1983.

Stylistically, this enormous group of portraits contains pieces of great diversity employing musical idioms already discussed with regard to earlier Thomson portraits. Therefore, I will simply comment upon some of the more unusual pieces from this group.

Lise Deharme: In a Bird Cage (42) is what Cage calls "le style oiseau."[40] This interesting virtuoso piano piece with its chromatic and whole-tone harmonic language will be analyzed in Chapter V. *Louise Ardant: With Trumpet and Horn (43)* is a piece suggestive of "hunting music",in which the the technical demands are such that it was included by Thomson in his collection of *Nine Etudes for Piano* from 1951.

Several portraits from this group are very contrapuntal and canonic, such as *Sophie Taüber-Arp (48), Georges Hugnet (46), Theodate Johnson: Invention (51), Howard Putzel (54),* and *Nicolas de Chatelain: Cantabile (62)*—an example of tertial counterpoint. Several portraits contain long passages of unremitting bitonal clash, including: *Pablo Picasso: Bugles and Birds (52)* which contains a long passage juxtaposing E-flat and E; *The Dream World of Peter Rose-Pulham (56)* which opposes D-flat and D at first sequentially, then in juxtaposition and also contains a waltz passage in E-flat accompanied by D; and *Mary Widney: Toccata (60)* which ruthlessly combines F-major and F-minor.

In his bitonal music in general, Thomson frequently combines tonalities that produce the most severe harmonic conflict, often juxtaposing passages in half-step relationships, or major/minor parallel relationships. Many com-

[40]Cage, *Virgil Thomson*, p. 184.

posers use the bitonal language to produce a type of layered, combinatory harmony. But, as I have suggested in the discussion of polyharmony, when Thomson employs bitonality he still writes primarily linearly. Since he wants to draw the listeners attention to the contrapuntal relationships of the two parts, he selects key relationships of severe contrast (frequently a half-step) thereby isolating them from each other.

Some of the portraits from 1940 are relatively straightforward tonal pieces structured with traditional sectional forms. Examples include: *Max Kahn: Fanfare for France (45)*, a strict, da capo ternary piece; *Tango Lullaby (50)*, another traditional ternary dance form; and the short, three-movement Piano Sonata No. 4, a portrait of Peggy Guggenheim called *Guggenheim Jeune (53)*, sketched by Thomson in two sitting sessions on two consecutive days in May, 1940. The Piano Sonata No. 4 was taken up by the eminent harpsichordist Sylvia Marlowe, who in 1951 became a subject for a Thomson portrait. Marlowe performed and recorded the *Guggenheim Jeune* portrait on the harpsichord, a practice followed by a distinguished pianist, the late Paul Jacobs, on the Nonesuch recording "Virgil Thomson: A Portrait Album," one of the last recordings made by Paul Jacobs before his untimely death in 1983.

By June of 1940 Thomson realized that not only for his own safety, but to help keep escape routes uncongested for endangered Europeans who might suddenly need them, he had to return to the United States. Travelling through the Pyrenees mountains in July, Thomson wrote the last three portraits of his European residency —*Comtesse de Forceville (63)*, *Jamie Campbell (64)*, and *André Ostier (65)*, all for piano. After returning to the United States in the late summer—while visiting the home of conductor Alexander Smallens in Stamford, Connecticut—he wrote the piano portrait *Alexander Smallens: Fugue (66)* and *Ruth Smallens (67)*, his last completed portrait for violin solo. The total number of portraits from the 1940 group was twenty-seven.

On October 10, 1940 Thomson was appointed music critic for the *New York Herald Tribune*, a position he would occupy with distinction for fourteen years. During the first few years of this period Thomson's pace of composition slowed down, at least in relationship to the very productive decade of the 1930s. He continued portrait writing in the early 1940s, but with less frequency. Of the four piano portraits composed between June and October of 1941, two are especially interesting. Cage points out that *Jessie K. Lasell: Percussion Piece (70)* uses, as do Thomson's next three choral works, fewer than seven tones; it is primarily pentatonic but contains segments of whole-tone scales and chords built with perfect fifths.[41] *Florine Stettheimer: Parades (71)* alternates passages of bitonal counterpoint—E-flat and D-major are mixed in the opening section—with passages that are literally musical "parades," one in ABA form. The collage-like structure of this piece will be analyzed in Chapter V.

[41]Ibid., p. 192.

About this time Thomson's portraits attracted the attention of conductor André Kostelanetz, who was hoping to commission some orchestral music for a series of guest appearances with various orchestras. Kostelanetz suggested the idea of making musical portraits of great Americans to three composers: Virgil Thomson, Aaron Copland, and Jerome Kern. Thomson's amusing account of the circumstances surrounding this commission is quoted below:[42]

> Kostelanetz suggested that I make a portrait of Eleanor Roosevelt. Well, Eleanor didn't have time. And then he suggested Mayor LaGuardia and Dorothy Thompson, the political columnist—he thought the two of them might equal Eleanor Roosevelt. And the Mayor said sure but I can't give him any time alone because I don't have time to see my wife alone! So I went to City Hall and wrote while he was administering the affairs of the city, and sketched this waltz. The Mayor's is a rather pleasant piece, one of those bumptious waltzes. But Dorothy's is a bunch of canons with Yankee Doodle in it. I don't know. I'm not so fond of that.

These pieces, which have not been published, represent the only two portraits that Thomson specifically conceived for full orchestra. For this same commission Copland wrote the *Lincoln Portrait*— which is not at all a portrait in the Thomson sense, but a very successful melodrama containing excerpts for narrator from Lincoln speeches with orchestral accompaniment—and Jerome Kern wrote one of his few orchestral compositions, the *Mark Twain Suite*.

Thomson's pleasure with these pieces contributed to his decision to orchestrate seven piano portraits two years later in 1944. Thomson is very enthusiastic about these orchestrated portraits which include: *Nicolas de Chatelain, Georges Hugnet, Flavie Alvarez de Toledo: Tango Lullaby*—all scored for strings, woodwinds, and bells; and *Jere Abbott, Pablo Picasso, Alexander Smallens*, and *Jessie K. Lasell*—all scored for full orchestra. Thomson has conducted these pieces and recorded three of them for Composers Recordings, Inc. (CRI-398E). In our discussions Thomson was particularly enthusiastic about Leopold Stokowski's performance of these pieces. Referring to the *Tango Lullaby* he said:[43]

> The *Tango Lullaby*, for instance, works a mile a minute for every kind of instrumentation. The orchestral version as played by Stokowski was out of this world. He really got it right.

Between July and October of 1942 Thomson wrote six additional piano portraits. Paul Bowles, the writer and composer, described this group, with a metaphor that would describe many others as well, as giving "the impression of having come from nowhere, airily in and out of the focus of consonance and dissonance like breezes through a pagoda."[44]

[42]Thomson, interview, March 16, 1982.
[43]Thomson, interview, January 25, 1982.
[44]Richard Jackson, "Virgil Thomson," *New Grove Dictionary*, XVIII, 788.

From this same group another portrait of special interest is *Aaron Copland: Persistently Pastorale (78).* This joyous, lyrical, G-major piece contains two large sections: an opening section of two-part, imitative counterpoint, and a concluding section employing parallel triads and thirds. In 1945, Thomson included this portrait in his film score for John Houseman's documentary *Tuesday in November.* To quote from Thomson's autobiography: "I used in this score, for expressing buoyant euphoria, my portrait of Aaron Copland."[45]

For the next nine years, from the completion of the Copland portrait in October of 1942 until 1951, Thomson wrote only two more portraits, both for piano. *Briggs Buchanan: Five-Finger Exercise (80),* written in August of 1943, is a fanciful, coloristic etude for white-notes only, and is included as one of Thomson's first set of piano etudes, *Ten Etudes for Piano (1943-44). Lou Harrison: Solitude (81),* from December of 1945, alternates sections of imitative counterpoint with passages of parallel, whole-tone intervals.

One of the contributing reasons for the absence of Thomson portraits during these years was his distraction with another major project, his second operatic collaboration with Gertrude Stein, *The Mother of Us All (1947),* Stein's last completed work. After this, until very recently Thomson turned only occasionally to portrait writing.

Thomson's second book of piano etudes, *Nine Etudes,* includes his next completed portrait as etude number seven, *Sylvia Marlowe: Chromatic Double Harmonies,* from June, 1951. (*Nine Etudes* also includes the 1940 *Louise Ardant* portrait, which Thomson decided was difficult enough to be appropriately included in a book of etudes.) *Chromatic Double Harmonies,* an interesting and difficult piece, presents a two-part contrapuntal texture, each part of which is composed of, to borrow Cage's phrase, "assorted three-note mutually exclusive aggregates."[46] The contrapuntal relationship between these two lines of aggregates contains passages in first, second, and third species formats, and cross-rhythms of three against two, and four against three. The difficulty of the piece results from the fact that a legato line must be distinguished in the right hand aggregates throughout the piece, as the opening measures and Thomson's directions indicate (Figure 6):

Figure 6.

[45]Thomson, *Virgil Thomson,* p. 357.
[46]Cage, *Thomson,* p. 223.

Thomson's ambitious, three-movement, thirteen-minute Concerto for Flute, Strings, Harp, and Percussion (83), written in 1954, is, Thomson maintains, a portrait of painter Roger Baker drawn from life. In our conversations, Thomson described the interesting and somewhat amusing procedure by which this long Flute Concerto/portrait was composed:[47]

> The Flute Concerto was done on three different days. We were, both Roger Baker and I, visiting in Mexico, visiting Carlos Chavez. He gave us a bedroom with a two-decker bed. I slept in the lower bed while Roger slept up top. I would compose in my bed while he was above drawing or something. Anyway, we were in the same room. He wasn't posing consciously, but they [the three movements] were his portrait and I knew it at the time. The orchestral score, naturally, was worked out later.

The Flute Concerto is the only Thomson portrait that is also a work of major proportions. A discussion of this piece is beyond the scope of this survey, but Cage devotes five pages of analysis to the Flute Concerto in his book.[48]

Hommage à Marya Freund (84) is a piano piece written in July of 1956. It is not a portrait drawn from life but a piece that after its completion Thomson decided to title a "Hommage" to this distinguished singer. However, this piece is listed in the catalog for the Virgil Thomson collection at the Yale library as a portrait, and was included by Thomson in the 1981 Boosey & Hawkes volume of portraits. As was mentioned previously, it was later transformed along with the Piano Sonata No. 2 into the Concertino for Harp, Strings, and Percussion from 1964. Similarly, *A Study in Stacked-Up Thirds* (85) from 1958 is a piano etude eventually dedicated to Eugene Ormandy on his seventieth birthday and not a portrait drawn from life. It too, however, is included in the Yale catalog as a portrait, and in the volume *Nine Portraits for Piano* published by Southern Music.

In December of 1966 Thomson wrote *Edges: A Portrait of Robert Indiana* (87), a piano portrait later arranged for band in 1969, and the *Portrait of Frederic James* (86), an etude for cello and piano and the only portrait for this instrumental combination. Therefore, for twelve years, from the composition of the Flute Concerto in 1954 until December of 1966, Thomson did not write any portraits drawn from life. Of course, during the years 1961-1968 Thomson was preoccupied with the composition of his third and most large-scaled opera *Lord Byron* (libretto by Jack Larson), which was premiered in New York in April, 1972 at the Julliard Opera Theatre.

The only portraits from the 1970s are the group of five commissioned by the American Brass Quintet called *Family Portrait* (88-92). Four members of one family and a "visitor" (metaphorically, not literally), Willy Eisenhart, are the subjects for these portraits, sketched for piano in August 1972 and scored two years later for the special technical facilities of the American

---

[47]Thomson, interview, March 16, 1982.
[48]Cage, *Thomson*, pp. 234-238.

Brass Quintet. The *Family Portrait* is a virtuoso brass suite of the first magnitude and a wonderful set of evocative, attractive portraits.

After Thomson's eightieth birthday in 1976, the pace of his composing understandably slackened but did not cease. Some recent larger compositions include: *Fanfare for Peace* for chorus with brass, and *The Cat* for vocal duo, 1981—both to texts of Jack Larson; *Thoughts for Strings*, 1981; and a *Cantantes Eamus* for male chorus and brass, commissioned by the Harvard Glee Club for their 125th Anniversary Concert in 1983. In the summer of 1981, the year of the numerous celebrations and festivities surrounding his eighty-fifth birthday, Thomson also returned to portrait writing with seeming abandon. From June of 1981 to the time of this writing (January, 1985), Thomson has added nearly fifty portraits to his list of works. The musical portrait genre still sustains Thomson's interest and considerable energy and he appears to have no intention of stopping them.

As a group, the recent Thomson portraits have typically diverse styles and musical idioms, but share some striking similarities. They are all relatively short (sixty to ninety seconds for the majority), linear pieces, possessing great continuity and evidencing much less interest on Thomson's part in juxtaposing contrasting sections of music in a collage-like manner, a featured technique of earlier portraits. The harmonic language ranges from straightforward diatonicism to fanciful, sometimes jarring polyharmony. Some are strict bitonal compositions, one even written with two different key signatures—*Bill Katz: Wide Awake* (93), in G-flat and G-major.

Many of these portraits are examples of direct, unsentimental, two-part polyphonic music. Much like the Inventions of Bach, they evolve simply and clearly, avoiding climactic moments. Some examples of this style include: *Norma Flender* (94), *Scott Wheeler:Free Wheeling* (96), *Barbara Epstein: Untiring* (102), *Anne-Marie Soullière: Something of a Beauty* (108), *Peter McWilliams: Firmly Spontaneous* (119), *Power Boothe: With Pencil* (121), and *Mark Beard: Never Alone* (122).

The manuscripts for the majority of the recent portraits contain very little in the way of dynamic indications, phrasings, and articulation marks. The tempo indications are clearly only Thomson's suggestions; the pieces "work," like the Bach Inventions, at virtually any tempo. However, what does abound in the scores are cautions regarding excessive expressiveness: "molto uguale," "senza espressione," "senza crescendo ni diminuendo," "abrupt." In one case, *Senza Espressione: Bennett Lerner* (126)—another portrait in this simple two-part texture—Thomson went so far as to write on the manuscript the following direction: "N.B. Please, no phrasing, no accents, no crescendo or diminuendo." These portraits are "elemental" musical compositions in the most sophisticated sense of the term and can not bear the weight of excessive expressiveness. I will have more to relate about issues of performance practice with respect to the portraits in Chapter V, in which I analyze another portrait from this group, *Richard Flender: Solid Not Stolid* (95).

This recent group also contains the two portraits for violin and piano previously referred to: *Cynthia Kemper: A Fanfare (118)*—a sturdy, attractive, three-part polyphonic fanfare in D, with the violin and piano treble line in strict canon at the octave; and *Lily Hastings (128)*—a three-part imitative polyphonic piece in A-flat major, which projects a curious quality of deliberate, decorative, meandering.

Two additional portraits of interest, commissioned in 1984, are: *Jay Rozen (131)*, for tuba and piano; and *A Portrait of Two: For Joelle Amar (130)*, for oboe, bassoon, and piano. The *Portrait of Two* is a complete three-movement composition of considerable vitality, intricacy, and charm. It was sketched from sittings on three successive days—Dr. Joell Amar sat on the first day, Benjamin Zifkin (the husband of Joelle Amar) sat on the second, and both of them on the third. The *Jay Rozen* portrait was commissioned by its subject, a graduate student from the Yale School of Music who raised money for this commission by advertising in a brass players' journal.

Thomson's present involvement with the portrait genre extends beyond composing. He has presided over the editing and publication of the recent portraits so that the majority are now available. As a result of a commission from the Oshkosh Symphony Orchestra, eleven portraits from 1981-82 have been orchestrated—five by Thomson, and three each by Boston composers Scott Wheeler and Rodney Lister, both former students and present colleagues of Thomson, both also subjects of Thomson portraits. This work, *Eleven portraits for Orchestra (1982)*, is now available on a recording, joining several other recent recordings of Thomson portraits for diverse ensembles. All specifics concerning these activities are listed in the thematic catalog section of this book.

One remaining issue with regard to this survey concerns the criteria by which the piano portraits have been selected and grouped together for publication in various editions. The first albums of Thomson piano portraits were published in four volumes by Mercury Music in 1948, 1949, 1950, and 1953 respectively, each containing eight portraits. (A fifth volume, though planned and listed in the bibliography of the Cage book, was in fact never published.) Had Thomson grouped the pieces together in any programmatic way or considered each volume to be a performing group? His comments follow:[49]

> AT: Did you make the selections and place the pieces in a predetermined order for the Mercury Music volumes?
>
> VT: I think I must have selected them. There were originally supposed to be five volumes and they got tired after four and never brought out the fifth. Now that was Mercury. When they sold their place to Presser's in Bryn Mawr I took them back and sold them to Schirmer's [the present publisher]. I didn't like Presser's. I have things at Presser's now because they have a new and much better management.

[49]Thomson, interview, March 16, 1982.

AT: Did you group them in volumes?

VT: I picked them out so as to make a pleasant distribution. I had some interesting numbers in each one.

AT: Is there any sense in which you conceived of them as a group that could be performed together?

VT: Well, they could be but there's no integrity in the grouping, you see. Ned Rorem, an old pupil of mine, and I have a war going on about this. He publishes groups of songs put together for convenience, or even for some kind of unity by the same poet or other, but he calls them cycles and I maintain they're not cycles at all, just groups. A cycle like *Frauenliebe und Leben* or *Die Winterreise* tells a kind of story. They are like Stations of the Cross or something. These portraits are just groups that could be played together or published together. I didn't want to have all the same kind of thing in one volume.

The volume of *Nine Portraits* published by Southern Music in 1974 and the *Thirteen Portraits* published by Boosey & Hawkes in 1981 are simply selections of various piano portraits that had not previously been published. The *Nineteen Portraits* published by Boosey & Hawkes in 1982 are all piano portraits dating from June 1981 to January 1982, and are grouped chronologically. Schirmer will soon publish another volume of *Seventeen Portraits*, containing the portraits from 1982-83, again grouped chronologically.

Since the vast majority of Thomson's portraits (over 100 of them) are for piano solo, there is one final issue of relevance to a stylistic survey—their degree of pianistic difficulty and their pianistic character. All of the Thomson piano portraits are the products of a composer with great understanding of piano sonority and technique. Thomson wrote two important books of etudes for piano that specifically address technical problems peculiar to twentieth century piano music, and the portraits demonstrate his understanding of the piano's capabilities.

The range of difficulty in the piano portraits is quite extreme. Some—for example, *Lise Deharme: In a Bird Cage*, *Alexander Smallens*, and the three portraits that are in fact etudes—are very demanding in terms of digital strength and independence, yet were conceived pianistically and contain few awkward passages. Some portraits are relatively elementary in their technical aspects. The majority make demands that would be characterized in the intermediate to advanced range.

Because Thomson composes away from a keyboard, many piano portraits—even those written in a straight forward, two-part contrapuntal texture—do not lie "in the fingers" comfortably. For example, *Peter McWilliams: Firmly Spontaneous (119)*, a two-part, contrapuntal study in 6/8 meter, contains arpeggios of sixteenth-notes in both hands, made more demanding by the ramdom octave doublings that punctuate both lines. Such writing is clearly fostered by Thomson's composing method; notes are not always determined by digital accessibility.

One of the motivations for the present study was a desire to call attention to an enormous body of distinctive, imaginative music for diverse instruments, but especially for the piano, containing many pieces with great programming potential most of which are now available in new editions. But many elementary to intermediate level Thomson portraits would make excellent teaching pieces as well. Editions of collected piano portraits, graded for difficulty and containing pictures and biographies of their subjects, would provide an excellent source of fresh pedagogical materials.

CHAPTER 5

Four Portraits:
An Analysis

In the previous chapters, the Thomson portraits were discussed as an entire group, with regard both to their general stylistic characteristics and the compositional method by which they were produced. Through an analytic discussion of four selected piano portraits, I will illustrate the specific musical results of Thomson's method, and will examine their stylistic features in theoretical detail. However, with regard to the choice of pieces for analysis, Thomson was not particularly helpful. When I asked him for recommendations of portraits, both for lecture-recital programs and for this analysis, he said: "I don't know one from another; after I've written them I don't think about them too much."[1]

As we have seen, many of the Thomson portraits are structured by means of relatively simple dance forms and other traditional musical forms (for example, the prelude and fugue, sectional forms, two-part contrapuntal forms); others are structured quite freely. However, in this chapter I have chosen to focus on the issue of musical continuity. There is a strong quality of linear continuity in even the non-repetitive, athematic portraits. In light of Thomson's spontaneous compositional method, the almost narrative quality of continuous line present in these portraits is all the more remarkable and deserving of analysis.

I have selected four portraits illustrative of different compositional idioms, but all possessing this quality of linear continuity. Two will be discussed in

[1]Thomson, interview, March 16, 1982.

some detail: *Alternations (14)*, with regard to the problem of pitch organization in the non-repetitive, collage-like portraits; and *Parades (71)*, with regard to Thomson's use of polyharmony. Two others will be discussed only briefly in terms of pitch organization, but have been included because of their special relevance to the pianist. *In a Bird Cage (42)* will be discussed with regard to issues of pianistic sonority, and *Richard Flender (95)*, with regard to performance practice issues applicable to all the Thomson portraits.

Alternations: A Portrait of Maurice Grosser (14),(reproduced here on pages 55, 56, and 57) written in PAᵣis on October 28, 1929, was Thomson's second portrait of Grosser. Thomson pointed to *Alternations* in our discussions as a particular example of the kind of "jerky continuity" discussed in Chapter IV:[2]

> Maurice's portrait, that's very jerky continuity, but you see, [laughs] he's a nervous type with a Jewish nervous system, very fast movements. A strong man with lots of integrity in his character and in his own continuity. But it doesn't look like continuity on the surface.

Even a cursory examination of this piece reveals it to be clearly sectional, the sections following either in abrupt succession or merged together with transitions. The piece begins with a flourish (mm. 1-3) of which Thomson has said, "This is a gypsy movement, the whole piece is drenched in Spain." [3] This introductory idea cadences in m.9 and leads into a distinctly different chordal section that ends abruptly in m.16. The next section, mm. 17-28 (in G, in 3/4 meter) is a gentle dotted-rhythm dance in a lyrical idiom, but it is succeeded by a larger section from mm. 29-46 in D flat which features, starting in m.31, piano chord alternations that give to the title its triple meaning: Grosser's character is one of alternations; the piece alternates sections of different music; and the two hands alternate sixteenth-note chords.

This D-flat section ends abruptly in m.46 and is succeeded by a section of rather simplistic two-part counterpoint, mm. 47-63. Another intrusive alternation of sixteenth-note major seconds (C-D) by both hands in mm. 65-65 leads to the ambiguous concluding section of the piece, mm. 66-82.

This distinctly sectional, non-repetitive piece has, for this listener, clear and strong continuity. One unifying device is the persistent use of a simple rhythmic dance pattern underlying the entire portrait:

This rhythm is sometimes followed by an additional measure with the following short/long pattern:

Because of the slight permutations of the figure, the frequently changing
meters, and the extremely contrasting content of the portrait's various sections, the strength of this rhythmic pattern as a unifying device is subliminal.
But the following chart shows the occurences and variations of this pattern
throughout the contrasting sections of this piece:

mm. 9-10

mm. 13-14

mm. 17-18

mm. 25-26

mm. 27-28

mm. 39-40

i.e. :

mm. 47-48

But the more complex unifying device concerns the pitch organization.
Alternations represents one of the many Thomson portraits with no clearly
premeditated pitch plan, unlike many of the tonal dances or character
pieces. Thomson literally did not know how this piece was going to evolve or
conclude, and any attempt by me to drawn him out on this subject elicited,
usually, a shouted response: "It just came out that way." Yet, though spontaneously and unconsciously conceived, *Alternations* contains a clear pattern of

pitch organization that contributes to the subliminal sense of continuity and cohesion in this collage-like piece.

Although most of the piece seems to project C as the tonal center, the sense of a clear tonal organization in *Alternations* is, in fact, ambiguous. I suggest that the tonal organization is based on a pattern of pitch relationships consisting of a configuration of thirds around E. These thirds occur in the piece both linearly and harmonically, and create an ambiguity where E is at times III of C, but also an alternative tonal center (Figure 7).

Figure 7.

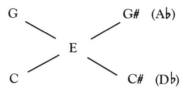

The C-E-G# augumented triad and the C#-E-G diminished triad are emphasized linearly and harmonically. The half-step relationships between Ab(G#) and G, and Db(C#) and C will also be seen to be crucial harmonically. At various moments in the piece there is a tonicization of all pitches in this configuration, except for G#(Ab). Also, the important thematic ideas in the piece are based on simple three-note, scale-step motives derived from this configuration: 3-2-1, in C, E, G, and Db.

The opening "Gypsy flourish" outlines a simple descending scale motive in C (mm. 1-4) and ends with a low intruding E octave (Figure 8):

Figure 8.

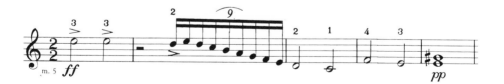

The next phrase (mm. 5-9) makes this more explicit (Figure 9):

Figure 9.

ALTERNATIONS: *A Portrait of Maurice Grosser**

VIRGIL THOMSON

*Reprinted by permission of G. Schirmer, Inc., N.Y.; copyright 1969.

Paris, October 28, 1929

16646

The E-major chord in m.9 is experienced as III of C, but then immediately tonicized by the subsequent passage. The motivic element of this passage is again the 3-2-1 scale idea—now in E-major and harmonized in the parallel chord "church style" of Thomson. (When I asked Thomson why the "church style" section occurs at this point he replied, "I can't tell you 'why' anything, but's its all perfectly true or I wouldn't have let it out of the house.") The striking chord progression in mm. 14-15, climaxing on an Ab major chord, is best understood as a movement from E up a third to G♯ (enharmonically Ab).

The progression of tonal centers so far has been from C to E to G♯(Ab), all major thirds. The fortissimo Ab-major harmony is clearly an implied Neapolitan-type chord descending by half-step to the piece's dominant area of G. The Ab area in the piece is always used as a Neapolitan-type relationship to G, a relationship implied in the pitch configuration chart (see Figure 7). The G-major scale in thirds which ends on the major third (Ab/C), m.16, is an abrupt ending to the first big section of the piece, an abrupt statement of the new tonal area, and a recapitulation of the Neapolitan progression in m.15, Ab to G.

The sense of continuity in the next section—the G-major episode in 3/4 meter starting at m.17—is achieved by the use of the motivic 3-2-1 scale-step material, and the use of parallel sixths in the right hand—the inversion of the parallel thirds from the church-style chordal section. (About this G-major section Thomson said, "I suppose that's Maurice in a quiet domestic mood, but none of it ever lasts very long.")[4]

The dotted-rhythm figure in m.17 initiates the increased rhythmic activity of this entire section. The harmonic rhythm also accelerates, but the harmonic progression is still based on thirds: from G, to E (m.25), to C♯ (m.26), back up to E (m.27), to Ab(G♯) (m.27), to B (m.28) and then finally by whole step to Db(C♯). This last shift, from B to Db(C♯), is the only significant harmonic progression in the piece by whole-step movement. D flat is now established as the temporary tonal center, but will not be totally clear until its half-step relationship with C (as is indicated in the pitch configuration chart) is established. There is a bass motion in mm. 35-39 that reestablishes D-flat as the tonal center by descending from Db to Cb to Bb, then up to C—the leading tone of Db (Figure 10)).

Figure 10.

m. 35

[4]Thomson, interview, March 16, 1982.

This section is the most diatonic and rhythmically dance-like in the piece and even contains a reference to what Cage has called Thomson's "signature tune," "For He's a Jolly Good Fellow" (mm. 29-35). Thomson concedes that he has on occasion quoted this tune, but only during a certain period and especially in the *Symphony on a Hymn Tune* from 1928.[5]

The section of chordal alternations (beginning in m.39 through m.46) can be heard as the intrusion of the Ab(G♯) area of the pitch configuration into the "jolly" world of Db-major. The previously observed function of Ab as a Neapolitan-type preparation for G is the specific function of Ab in this climactic passage (except that Ab at its first intrusion in m.39 is both in minor mode, and incomplete—implied by only its upper third, Cb and Eb). It is first answered with the "wrong" scale in thirds—G-minor—which climaxes deceptively on the major third Db-F, in m.42 (an analogous passage to the G-major scale in m.16). The subsequent passage of chord alternations is the simple chromatic filling-out of a dramatic Neapolitan-type preparation for a G-major chord (V of C) that finally appears in m.46 (Figure 11).

Figure 11.

m. 42   N (Ab)—G

Cage describes the subsequent section of two-part counterpoint in C (mm. 47-57) as "purposefully inept." [6] Thomson's description of Grosser's character—a "nervous. type with a Jewish nervous system, very fast movements"—does not call to mind the sense of "internal organization" in people that he unconsciously mimicks in strict polyphonic portraits. Therefore, Cage's description of this humorous passage seems quite appropriate.

The continuity of this section with the rest of the portrait is based on the previously described rhythmic pattern:

and the simple motivic 3-2-1 scale patterns. There is a rhythmically emphasized linear progression to the tonic C in contrary motion between both hands in mm. 55-62 that is outlined in Figure 12 below:

[5]Thomson, interview, March 16, 1982.
[6]Cage, *Virgil Thomson*, p. 163.

Figure 12.

Figure 13.

The contrary motion scales imply a simple V7 of C and converge on the major second (C-D) in m.64, which implies either the dominant preparation of ii7, or V7/V in C (Figure 13):

But on the downbeat of m.66 appears the first A-major chord of the piece. When the seventh is added to this chord in the second beat, the resulting linear reference is to the pitch configuration chart: (A)-C♯-E-G. But the jarring F octave in m.67, reminiscent of the E octave in m.4, is a surprise and sets up a different expectation.

The one harmonic area of C-major that has been neglected so far in this piece is the sub-dominant area of F. I propose that with respect to tonality, this very curious and ambiguous concluding section of *Alternations* suggests a dramatic, unprepared tonal shift to F, of which the III area would be A. Linearly and vertically, the passage from mm. 67-71 implies F major on the basis of the following: the V7 chord of F in m.68; the scale-step motion in mm.68-70, both ascending in the right hand (B♭, C, D, E, to an implied F), and descending in the bass (C, B♭, A, G, to an implied F). But, in m.72 the bass line in fact descends to F♯. The augmented triad at that moment (F♯-A-C) reminds the listener of the augmented triad from the original pitch configuration chart (C♯-E-G), except that the entire configuration pattern is now centered around F instead of E.

The tonal clarity of the right hand line in mm. 73-76 (scale-steps 3-2-1 in C) is undermined by an ambiguous bass pattern implying first C (mm. 73-74), then F (m.75), then E-minor (m.76), and finally resting on a chord in m.77, B♭-F-C, voiced so as to project its two perfect fifths. The piece concludes by linearly and vertically restating the original pitch configuration of thirds: first C-E-G♯ in the sixteenth-note alternation in mm. 77-78; then

C♯-G in m.79. Only the E is missing. After a whole measure of rest, an E octave is struck at triple pianissimo in the bass, recapitulating both the bass E octave in the opening measures and its resulting sense of ambiguity.

The overall harmonic structure of *Alternations* can be explained in C major, but the ending makes clear that the configuration of thirds around E is the organizational device that is responsible for all the harmonic, motivic, and tonal events of this piece. But this pitch configuration also contributes to the successful (though subliminal) sense of continuity in this portrait, and to the imaginative ambiguity of its character.

Florine Stettheimer: Parades (71),(reproduced her on pages 62 through 65) written in New York on October 5, 1941, is an examplem of Thomson's use of bitonality. With regard to the title of this portrait Thomson explained:[7]

> Well, Florine's studio was a block away from Fifth Avenue, and Fifth Avenue is full of parades. It's as if you were always hearing parades going by in the back of your mind.

The quality of parades evoked "in the back of your mind" is achieved in this portrait primarily by its particular tonal language. Although Thomson has written many strict bitonal pieces—for example, *Bill Katz: Wide Awake* (93), written with two key signatures (G♭-major and G-major)—*Parades* is a more representative example of Thomson's bitonal writing, wherein passages of strict bitonality are juxtaposed with simple chordal polyharmony and with passages in diatonic keys. At any moment in *Parades* one tonal center usually dominates the texture, the added tonalities being used for coloristic dissonance or ambiguity, rarely creating the harsh conflict of two distinct keys. The vast majority of chords in this portrait are major triads in root position, each one distinctly audible. The predominant chord relationship is by the third—especially I to Major III, I to Major VI, and I to the lowered Major VI (or ♭VI). Also common to this piece is the use of motivic lines that move through different keys.

The structure of this piece, however, presents little ambiguity and is articulated clearly by its thematic, rhythmic, textural, and bitonal content. There is a distinct succession of four "parade" pieces with a final coda, the formal outline of which can be diagrammed as follows:

I. 3/4 meter; polyphonic (two parts); binary form.
    A   (mm. 1-8) eight measures.
    B   (mm. 9-16) eight measures.

II. 2/4 meter; homophonic; ternary form.
    A   (mm. 17-24) eight measures.
    B   (mm. 25-32) eight measures.
    A'   (mm. 33-40) eight measures.

[7]Thomson, interview, March 16, 1982.

Florine Stettheimer: Parades*

Virgil Thomson

*Reprinted by permission of Boosey and Hawkes, N.Y.; copyright 1981.

BH.BK.821

New York, October 5, 1941

BH.BK.821

III. 3/4 meter; polyphonic (two parts); binary form.
    A   (mm. 41-48) eight measures.
    B   (mm. 49-56) eight measures.
    trans. (mm. 57-60) four measures.

IV. 4/4 meter; polyphonic (three parts); ternary form.
    A   (mm. 61-68) eight measures.
    B   (mm. 69-72) four measures.
    A'   (mm. 73-80) eight measures.
    CODA (mm. 81-89) nine measures.

The categorization of the transition section and the coda is, of course, open to interpretation, but the obvious formal scheme of binary and ternary forms with basically eight-measure phrases seems indisputable.

Section I, phrase A (mm. 1-8), in two-part counterpoint, presents a treble line in D with a bass line in E-flat. However, the D-major line, with its drone-like repetition of scale degrees 3 and 5, dominates the texture. The Eb half-note in the bass line at every downbeat (for the first five measures) sounds almost like an "off pitch" drum. There is no linear definition of E-flat major, and no D-natural leading tone. Perfect fifths between the two voices are used as points of cadence (m.4, m.8; third beats), and because of the Eb-F-G-A whole-tone line in mm. 7-9 in the bass, the expectation is for the A-E perfect fifth (m.9) to resolved to D-major, which the bass, in fact, does. But the treble E resolves "incorrectly" up a step to F-Db (see Figure 14), keeping the interval relationship between the keys a half-step, but moving it down from the Eb-D of the opening to D-Db for phrase B.

Figure 14.

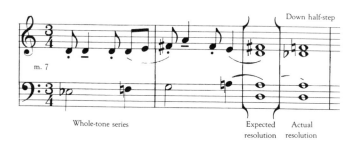

Phrase B (mm. 9-12) is dominated tonally by the new D-flat major treble line, partly because of its insistent rhythmic pattern:

which Boston composer Charles Fussell has called Thomson's "Kansas City cowboy rhythm."[8] The treble line (mm. 13-16) projects a sense of tonal transition, implying per measure the keys of Db, C, Bb, then (down a third to) G in m.17.

Section II is an ABA march in 2/4. The treble line is a steady, G major "bugle call," accompanied by the bitonally more consonant key of D-major, using the root-position triads of I, flat VI, I, and flat III (D, Bb, D, and F, respectively).

In the B phrase of section II (mm. 25-32) the "bugle call" down a third to E-major, the Major VI of G. The measure preceding phrase B (m.24) employs another "deceptive" harmonic transition similar to the one described in m.9. The chord on the second beat of m.24 (F major) implied a Neapolitan-type preparation for E-major (Figure 15).

Figure 15.

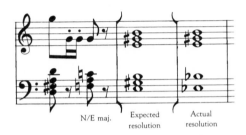

The "incorrect" resolution down a half-step to an Eb-Bb perfect fifth is made to seem more out of place by its subsequent alternation with A-major (m. 26, m. 28), the "correct" sub-dominant of melody's primary key (E major)—the "bugle-call" tune which dominates this phrase.

Phrase A', the third phrase of section II (mm. 33-40), mimics the G-major "bugle call" of the first A phrase (mm. 17-24), both by motivic similarity and by the use of a more consonant bitonal vocabulary. In fact, the series of chords in mm. 37-40 that results from this harmonic mixing could be analyzed as simple seventh chords in G-major (Figure 16).

Figure 16.

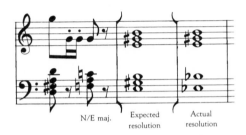

[8]Charles Fussell, interview, Cambridge, Massachusetts, March 18, 1982.

The E♭ seventh chord in m.40 suggest an augmented sixth chord in G, and although there is no stated dominant D (following the augmented sixth preparation) the tonic G is carried in the treble into the next section of the piece.

Section III (mm. 40-56) is a binary form passage that returns to 3/4 meter, and to the two-part polyphonic texture of Section I. The thematic material of phrase A (mm. 41-48) is similar enough to section I to suggest for the whole piece an overall structure of:

I II III IV: CODA
A B A' Finale: C-Major

The use of strict root position triads in phrase B (mm. 49-56) enforces the projection of two distinct lines intended to be heard polyphonically and not as vertical polychords (for example, mm. 53-54). The tonally ambiguous four-measure transition (mm. 57-60) suggested a lowered, or flat VI (A♭-major) preparation for both the dominant G (m.60) and for the subsequent concluding section of the piece in C-major.

Section IV is the most clearly delineated "parade," being a ternary form in 4/4, the A phrase of is a passage of three-part counterpoint suggesting the tune of "Yankee Doodle" (mm. 61-68). The B phrase (mm. 69-72) is a homophonic fanfare in C, and the A' phrase (mm. 73-80), an altered recapitulation of phrase A.

The interesting fanfare coda has a linear continuity and logic that overrides the polyharmonic vertical sonorities. The treble fanfare simply alternates C-major (I) and A-major (VI) until the dominant G-major chord (V) in m.86. The bass fanfare can best be explained linearly. The spelling of the triads in mm. 81-82 suggests that Ab-major is an upper neighbor chord, and G♭ a lower neighbor chord to the dominant G-major. The respelling of the Ab triad as G♯ in m.83 suggests that it is the dominant of C♯ which does appear in m.85, creating a C-major/C♯-major "confusion" similar to the piece's opening. The motion in the bass line (mm. 85-86) descends by fourths (a new interval of harmonic movement in this piece) from C♯, to G♯(A♭), to E♭, to B♭. This bass motion strongly suggests that the next step would be the subdominant chord of F, which does appear in m.88, but simultaneously with the dominant of G (in the treble line), thereby ending the piece with a IV+V chord and no tonic I.

The score of *Parades* that is published in the 1981 Boosey & Hawkes edition represents a slight revision of the first version, published originally in the January, 1943 issue of *View* magazine.[9] The general direction of the three changes in the new version is to make harmonic and structural events even more pronounced. One change concerns the tonic-less ending described

[9]Virgil Thomson, "Portrait of Florine Stettheimer," *View Magazine*, Series 2 No. 1 (January 1943): 49.

above. The *View* edition of these last measures omits measure 87 of the revised version (Figure 17).

Figure 17.

Bass motion by fourths

The revision adds a measure of tonic C octaves, resulting in an unexpected cadential scale degree movement of 1-2-5-(1, implied), and thereby increasing the sense of incompletion which results from the absence of a final tonic (Figure 18).

Figure 18.

The new edition contracts an eight-measure fanfare phrase of quarter-notes and half-notes into a much more rhythmically active, eighth-note, syncopated, four-measure phrase (mm. 69-72), used in both versions as phrase B of Section IV. Finally, the delineation of section II from section III is made more explicit by the addition of an extra quarter note as a stopping point in m.40 (Figure 19).

Figure 19.

View version   Boosey and Hawkes (1981 revision)

In 1970, *Parades* was revised again and transcribed for orchestra for the
occasion of a ceremony in New York honoring American painters. This
version was entitled *Metropolitan Museum Fanfare: Portrait of an American Artist*. Although the basic structure of *Parades* is unaltered in this orchestral
transcription, this version represents a total transformation of the piece involving a harmonic language much richer in whole-tone scales and the resulting augmented triads. In fact, the orchestral transcription (see catalog
listing no. 70), though very interesting, is more accurately viewed as a different composition based on this portrait and not merely an orchestration.

In a Bird Cage: Lise Deharme(42), (reproduced here on pages 72 and 73)
written in 1941, will be analyzed briefly, particularly with respect to
Thomson's use of coloristic piano sonorities. However, this piece also
manifests an interesting adaptation of the whole-tone scale, a strict
two-section formal scheme, and an unusual textural quality that all merit
some comment.

Concerning Lise Deharme and her portrait, Thomson explained:[10]

> Lise Deharme was a French woman poet who lived in a handsome Paris flat on
> the Place des Invalides. Her drawing room was a bird cage with birds actually
> flying around in it.

From Thomson's description it is clear that this piece is not only a portrait of
Lise Deharme, but also the unusual drawing room in which Madame Deharme entertained. The inclusion in some Thomson portraits of the sur-
roundings and ambiance in which his subjects are observed is not surprising,
coming as it does from a noted composer of film scores, incidental music,
and landscape pieces (for example, *Wheat Field at Noon*, *The Seine at Night*).

This breathless, brilliant, impressionistic portrait captures its subject most
successfully, yet is formally organized in a surprisingly appropriate two-
section structure. The piece is divided into an A section (mm. 1-10), and an
A¹ section of equal length (mm. 11-22) that repeats the first four measures of
section A exactly. For the first four measures the texture involves only a

---

[10]Thomson, interview, March 16, 1982.

single line, which then divides in m.5, both voices continuing in alternation until the concluding two measures of section A. The textural pattern is mimicked almost exactly in section A¹.

There is a strong rhythmic pattern and continuity in this piece characterized by a slow (quarter note = 60mm) but strongly emphasized common-time pulse, subdivided almost exclusively into either pairs of eighth-notes, groups of six sixteenth-notes, or eight thirty-second-notes.

The pitch organization is based in part on an interesting adaptation of a whole-tone scale with descending half-step alterations to indicate and identify the tonality of A (Figure 20).

Figure 20.

The descending half-step interruption from E♯ to E relates back to D♯, making the three-note pattern (D♯-E♯-E) sound like lower and upper auxiliary tones to E. This is also true of the G♯-A♯-A pitch group (Figure 21).

Figure 21.

The vertical arrangements of this linear material produce the following harmonic interval configurations (Figure 22), all used in this piece:

Figure 22.

The other important and closely related intervalic elements in this piece is the tritone B-F, used in its auxiliary relationship to the perfect fifth A-E. The

IN A BIRD CAGE: *A Portrait of Lise Deharme*[*]

VIRGIL THOMSON

194

con Pedale secundo

Paris, April 8, 1940

194

73

B-F tritone is drawn from the fifth and ninth of the dominant ninth chord on E (Figure 23), and it is always used as an evocation of the dominant harmony. But its larger identity is as a pair of upper auxiliary tones to the implied perfect fifth A-E, which is made clear in the opening thematic material (Figure 24).

Figure 23.

Figure 24.

This opening motive presents both the B-F tritone and the D♯-B♭ augmented third in such a way that implies their function as auxiliary notes to a resolution on the perfect fifth A-E.

The altered whole-tone scale is used in association with the A harmonic minor scale with a raised fourth degree—sounding almost like a leading tone to the fifth scale degree (E). This scale is first presented in beats three and four of m.3 (Figure 25).

Figure 25.

These altered harmonic minor scales and altered whole-tone scales alternate in the playful passage at mm. 7-8, introduced by the augmented sixth (Bb-G♯) in the bass clef.

Both section A and section A′ of this portrait end with linearly derived passages leading to the A-E perfect fifth. The passage ending section A (mm. 9-10) is heard as two step-wise chromatic lines converging on E (Figure 26).

Figure 26.

m. 11

Similarly, the final passage of this piece is comprised of a prolongation of the simple D♯-E♯-E auxiliary configuration, and a step-wise bass descent to A. The treble line at m.16 simply repeats scale degrees 4-3-4 (D♯-C♯-D♯) from the altered whole-tone scale, followed by the F from the B-F tritone in m.18 (enharmonically equivalent to the E♯ from the altered whole-tone scale), and resolving in m.20 to the E in the bass. (This represents in part a prolongation of the initial D♯-E♯-E configuration.) The bass line at m.17 states, enharmonically, the same auxiliary configuration (F-E♭-F-E), but is then followed by a descending step-wise filling-in of the F-B tritone before its final resolution to the A-E perfect fifth (Figure 27).

The final flourish in m.20 recapitulates all the pitch material: in the bass, the A-E perfect fifth; and in the treble, the G♯-A♯ (as auxiliary notes of A) in the first and last pitches of the thirty-second note figure; the B-F tritone; the E♭(D♯)-F(E♯)-E auxiliary configuration—with the dissonant E♭ and the consonant E left sustaining above the perfect fifth.

Figure 27.

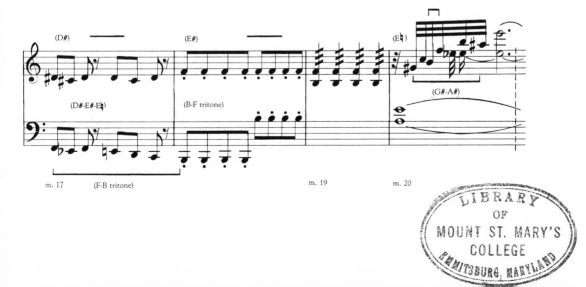

m. 17   (F-B tritone)   m. 19   m. 20

This portrait is especially interesting with regard to the unusual quality of the piano writing. The interesting aspect of the piano sonority in *In a Bird Cage* is the fact that many of the coloristic effects mimic special idiomatic technical devices of string instruments. This is especially true of the alternating melodic and harmonic interval repetitions which occur in three places—mm. 4, 14, and 19. The example from m.4 is quoted below (Figure 28):

Figure 28.

In this example, Thomson evokes the different possibilities of instrumentation for the measured tremolo on the violin and the contrasting sonorities that result.

The passage of alternating altered whole-tone and minor scales (mm. 7-8) employs an interesting pedal device. The descending altered minor scales are pedaled through, while the ascending whole-tone scales are not pedaled. The more ambiguous tonal material, the whole-tone scales, are thereby executed more clearly, while the more clearly diatonic minor scales are blurred. These blurred chromatic passages of thirty-second notes are also evocative of virtuoso string writing.

In addition, with regard to the piano an extreme registral spectrum is employed in this portrait, including—at the climax of the descending D-minor scale in m.6—the lowest note of the piano keyboard. Finally, the last chord of this piece is a beautiful sustained sonority produced by means of the sostenuto pedal, which prolongs the A-E perfect fifth while the dissonant Eb and the consonant E (as has been mentioned) are extracted out of this thirty-second note flourish and sustained (see Figure 28).

It is not surprising that this piece has been transcribed twice for string instruments: first by Luigi Silva in 1942 for cello and piano, and then by Samuel Dushkin in 1947 for violin solo. Both versions involve extensive use of string sonic sound effects, especially harmonics and pizzicati. The cello and piano version is faithful to the structure and notes of the original but divides single lines between the two instruments and employs a great expansion of register. The violin solo version interpolates two cadenza-like passages, one in particular involving a great prolongation and registral expansion of the B-F tritone from m.19 of the original. Thomson's pleasure with both transcriptions is indicative of the fact that *In a Bird Cage* is a piece of great color and sonority clearly evocative of string writing and string color and appropriate game for string transcriptions.

On one occasion Thomson listened to me play, amongst other pieces of his, the portrait *Richard Flender: Solid Not Stolid (950,* (reproduced here on page 78) written in 1981. His comments concerning this piece and my performance of it constitute a virtual summary of his performance practice ideas and are relevant not only to his piano portraits but, in some degree, to all his music. After a brief analysis of this more recent portrait, I will recount Thomson's comments regarding performance practice issues in his piano music.

Richard Flender presents a texture of intermingling linear and vertical elements in a particularly striking way. On one level this piece is conceived as two contrapuntal lines of parallel harmonic intervals, featuring a series of fourths against single notes (mm. 1-4), fourths against fourths (mm. 11-13), sixths against sixths (mm. 14-15), and more intervalically varied lines. In an inadvertent remark during one meeting, Thomson confirmed his intervalic, linear conception of this piece. When pressed by me about the construction of the chords, Thomson replied: "I don't know why it all came out lines of fourths, but it just did!"[11]

This polyphonic texture of intermingling lines of parallel intervals can be seen clearly in the passage from mm. 16-19. Each line has a clear linear harmonic identity and both move according to the simple principles of voice leading. However, this piece also projects a vertical texture that is harmonic. In fact, the basic harmonic materials of this portrait could be considered as the series of ninth chords in the key of D-major (Figure 29).

Figure 29.

| I9 | ii9 | iii9 | IV9 | V9 | vi9 | viio9 |

As voiced by Thomson, every chord in this piece is projected as implying a seventh, or ninth chord, or a chord of suspension all demanding resolutions to D-major. This characteristic of the harmony persists until the final chord of the piece (m.31), the only complete D-major chord.

The following example should clarify the harmonic interpretation of this primarily linear piece. The opening measures are quoted below with the implied chords of origin shown in the lower staff (Figure 30):

[11]Thomson, interview, March 16, 1982.

RICHARD FLENDER: Solid, Not Stolid*

Virgil Thomson

East Hampton, L. I., June 21, 1981

*Reprinted by permission of Boosey and Hawkes, N.Y.; copyright 1983.

Figure 30

The first chord of m.1 can be analyzed as comprising the root, fifth, and seventh of the iii7 of D, going to the V7, and implying a resolution to the tonic D major (Figure 30-a). But the specific voicing of the major ninth (E-F#) implies another interpretation (Figure 30-b): the first chord of m.1 is a ii9 (E- minor ninth chord) with a lowered seventh (D lowered to C#) in anticipation of the implied V7 that follows. This is a more fussy harmonic explanation, but seems more appropriate to the specifics of the voicing.

The chord in the second beat of m.2 can similarly be interpreted as a vii7 chord (Figure 30-c), or a V7 chord implying a 2-1 (B-A) suspension (Figure 30-d). But the main point is that all these chords, though they do not resolve in the context of the phrase, imply the tonality of D-major.

The ambiguity created by lines of intervals that indentify different harmonies both vertically and linearly is a characteristic of this entire piece and can be demonstrated in the following passage from m.5 (Figure 31):

Figure 31.

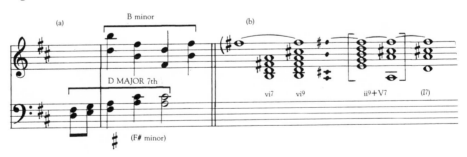

The treble line has a clear linear identity as B-minor, the bass line as a D7 chord. Yet even these linearly conceived lines have a vertical harmonic explanation (Figure 31-b). The chord on the first beat of m.5 can be analyzed as vi7 of D, the chord on the second beat as vi9. The chord on the third beat, a linear chord resulting from the crossing of two voices, implies a type of polychord: ii9 (E- minor ninth) plus V7 (A dominant seventh) in D-major. The implied but unstated resolution to D-major is also shown in Figure 31-b. There is an interesting quality in this example whereby the F♯—common to all the chords and projected strongly by the two perfect fifths in the treble (B-F♯)—seems to be prolonged throughout this progression, as suggested in Figure 31-b.

The upward resolution of the suspension (4-5) in the final chord of the piece (m.31) supports the interpretation of all harmonies in this portrait as linearly derived seventh and ninth chords implying resolutions to D-major. It is as if the final chord fulfills the implied expectations of all the previous chords in the piece.

In my performance of the piece for Thomson, I attempted to articulate the phrasing in a lyrical manner and to shape the piece by means of dynamic contours (the manuscript contained no dynamic indications). My intention was to compensate for the austerity of the texture and the stark harmony. This approach to the portrait was quite contrary to Thomson's intentions. He remarked that in performing, "there is a whole list of things you don't do that is even more important than what you do." He then continued:[12]

> All of my music, and particularly my keyboard music, is influenced by my long experience as an organist and my love of sustained sounds. You are making crescendos and diminuendos that are not written in. You are not playing it straight. You are putting in hairpins. You are opening and shutting the swell-box all the time. Play it straightforwardly. When a phrase ends just lift your fingers. But don't make a diminuendo. There is a special way this should sound—without any expression. Play it as though it were an organ piece.

It is clear that Thomson is referring as much to the drier, dynamically levelled, austere quality of expression associated with organ music as to the specific quality and sustaining power inherent in its sound. Many of the portraits, especially the piano portraits, are relatively simple in content, texture, and technique. Excessive expressivity undermines the sturdy simplicity that Thomson intended.

This started a discussion of the tempo of this portrait, which—as is common with the recent portraits—is not indicated on the copy of the manuscript from which I learned it. Thomson stated the following:[13]

> The tempo of contrapuntal music can change. Find the tempo at which you can play the hardest passages comfortably and that's it.

Most of the published Thomson portraits, including the contrapuntal ones, and even some of the unpublished recent ones have metronome markings,

---

[12]Thomson, interview, March 16, 1982.
[13]Ibid. [14] Ibid.

some with no other tempo indications. Does the performer have the same freedom with regard to tempi when there is an indicated metronome marking? Thomson's remarks concerning this issue are quoted below:[14]

> VT: Oh, those [the metronome indications] are done afterwards. As a matter of fact, with any musical composition of a spontaneous nature you just let it go along and then afterwards you treat it as if it were something by somebody else. You find a good tempo for it, make some good phrase marks, things like that.
>
> AT: Are the metronome marks for the published portraits accurate?
>
> VT: Nothing is accurate.
>
> AT: Many of them seem quite fast to me.
>
> VT: Fast? Could be. Could be.
>
> AT: For example, *Anne-Marie Soullière (108)*. What I think you want to be lively, at that tempo (3/4 meter; dotted-half note $=$ 72) gets a little hysterical. A little wild.
>
> VT: Could be. There is something about my piano music which I only discovered in coaching pianists to play it. Just as when I write music I have to let my mind alone—that's what I call the discipline of spontaneity—the performer has to learn to let his musical education alone and not superimpose the kind of expressive style that is conventional for, shall we say, romantic music. The whole business is, it's like setting words to music. You make the grammar, the syntax, the form, make all that clear and forget about expression. Make the articulation clear; and in order to do that you have to kind of orchestrate the music. I say "kind of" because it isn't a literal orchestration, but it's damn close to it.

My own impression from examining the portraits was that as a group many of them had metronome markings that seemed to be quite fast, some of them impossibly fast. It is clear that in an attempt to prevent performers from playing his portraits—especially the simpler, more contrapuntal ones, or those evocative of dance forms and character pieces—in an overly romantic, expressive manner, Thomson has indicated relatively fast metronome markings at which tempi sentimentality would be impossible. It is my judgment on this issue from our discussion of it that the metronome markings are there as a warning against excessive expressivity as much as an indication of tempo, and they can be reasonably modified if the warning is heeded.

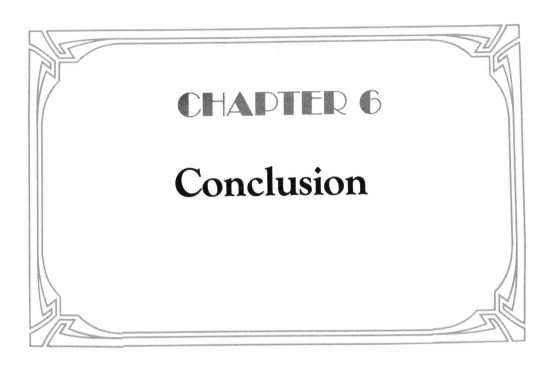

CHAPTER 6

Conclusion

This study has tried to demonstrate that, in part, the Thomson portraits represent exercises in broad characterization through the abstract medium of music. Inevitably, the listener to the portraits tries to extract from these pieces images of the personalities and characters of their subjects, not their composer. After performing a group of Thomson portraits during some recitals in 1981, I was asked by several students whether I knew Richard Flender, for, as one put it, he "must be so weird and interesting." But Thomson, as has been stated, makes no excessive claims for the success of these pieces as portraits. He personally believes that, to varying degrees, the portraits are successful character depictions, but accepts that for others this will be a subjective reaction and that ultimately they will be and must be judged for their intrinsic musical merit.

But this study has also tried to demonstrate that the 140 Thomson musical portraits represent his experiments with a spontaneous method of composition that is quite unique in music. With regard to this issue, Samuel L. M. Barlow, in an article for *Modern Music*, has stated that the portrait genre has "uses and designs," but cautions that this type of musical portraiture:[1]

[1]Samuel L. M. Barlow, "American Composers, XVII: Virgil Thomson," *Modern Music* 18 (May-June 1941):246.

. . .aids the facility and the memory, but it may induce a certain chucking of the Muse under the chin and it may so captivate the fancy of the author that, as in certain lapses on the part of Picasso, the striving platitude or the experimental charade gets hung with the masterpieces.

This particular "lapse" is not characteristic of Virgil Thomson who in an article for *Antaeus* in 1976 wrote:[2]

Unless the [portrait] turns out to be a whole piece and embodies what I esteem on later examination to be a good musical idea, I treat it as a painter would an unsuccessful effort. I discard it.

[2]Virgil Thomson, "Of Portraits and Operas," *Antaeus* 21/22 (Spring/Summer 1976):210.

PART II

Virgil Thomson's Musical Portraits:

A Thematic Catalog

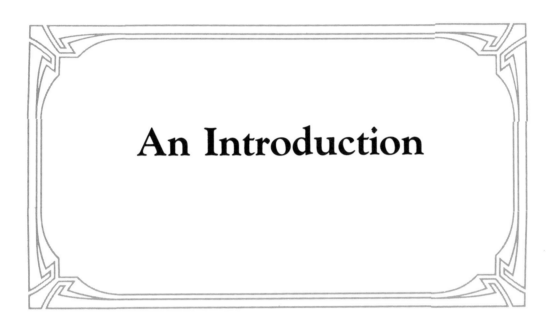

An Introduction

The following thematic catalog is the result of the best efforts of this writer to obtain the most current and accurate information (as of this writing—March 1985) about the entire canon of musical portraits by Virgil Thomson. Much information has been solicited directly from Virgil Thomson, especially with regard to the exact chronology of the portraits and the identities of their subjects. Thomson's comments—quoted extensively throughout this catalog—are personal reminiscences, always informative and often quite witty. To preserve the conversational vernacular of Thomson's remarks, I have with few exceptions quoted them exactly. All quotes are taken from my frequent taped conversations with Mr. Thomson, held between January, 1982 and January, 1985, in New York City, Boston, and Brookline, Massachusetts.

Much of the information in this catalog was gathered from the Virgil Thomson Collection at Yale University. In 1978, Yale acquired the manuscripts and papers of Virgil Thomson, an acquisition made possible, in part, by funds from the Booth Ferris Foundation. The Thomson papers and correspondences (over 40,000 pages of them) were the gift of Mr. Thomson, as were copies of his books and over 100 published scores.

The catalog for the Yale Collection was prepared under Thomson's supervision by Victor Cardell, a graduate of Trinity College with a M.L.S. degree from New York University. Cardell worked for Thomson in New York between 1974-1976 and is currently the Assistant Music Librarian for the John Herrick Jackson Music Library at Yale. An index to the collection, prepared by Jay Rozen, is housed at Jackson Library, but the documents and scores are housed in the Yale's Beinecke Rare Book and Manuscript Library (also the location of Yale's collection of the manuscripts and papers of Gertrude Stein).

The original manuscripts for the musical portraits and other compositions composed by Thomson since 1978 are still, with some exceptions, in the possession of the composer. The Yale Library has received photocopies of all these portraits which are in the process of being catalogued and added to the collection.

Additional information in this catalog has been gathered from the following sources:

1. Thomson's private catalog of his own music.
2. Photocopies of recent portraits given directly to me by Virgil Thomson.
3. Letters and correspondences with associates and friends of Virgil Thomson, including many portrait subjects.
4. General bibliographic reference sources.

The thematic catalog presented in this book contains seven categories of information. Descriptions of and abbreviations for each category will now be explained.

1. TITLE

All portraits that have been published are identified in this catalog by the titles that appear in the published versions. I discovered instances where the published titles differed from those listed in Thomson's own catalog. In such cases Mr. Thomson indicated that the published title should take precedence. For the unpublished portraits I have provided the title from Thomson's catalog, or, in a few very recent cases, the manuscript copy.

2. INCIPIT

Incipits—quotations from the opening measures of a piece—are provided for the traditional purpose, namely, absolute identification of a piece. With respect to the majority of piano portraits, only the opening treble clef line is quoted. When, in my judgment, the character of a piece is grossly misrepresented without inclusion of the bass clef part, I have quoted both clefs. In some instances, the opening bass clef part is so minimal as to be easily included in the treble clef incipit and I have done so. "L. H. tacet" is used to indicate that there is no bass clef part for the duration of the incipit. With respect to the portraits scored for various instrumental ensembles, I have used my judgment to determine the incipit.

3. DATE

The portraits are listed in chronological order. Specific dates of composition are taken from the original manuscripts, the listings in the Yale catalog, and the photocopies of recent manuscripts given to me by Mr. Thomson. In the few instances where the month and year is given but no specific day, and in the four instances where Thomson composed two portraits on one day, the chronology has been determined on the basis of Thomson's own recollections. (These instances are identified in the catalog.)

4. SCORING

The original scoring for each portrait is listed first, followed by any subsequent published transcriptions for other instruments by Thomson or other composers. I have also included the unpublished transcriptions by other composers of which I am aware.

5. SUBJECT

As I have argued, on one level the Thomson portraits are intended by the composer to be genuine attempts at character depiction. Accordingly, for the benefit of both performers and listeners, I have provided information to identify the subjects of all the portraits (except for certain internationally renowned figures—for example, Picasso). In many instances, I have provided biographical information, obtained either by my own research or submitted directly to me by the subject or an acquaintance of the subject. I have personally communicated with the majority of the, as Mr. Thomson has put it, "still available sitters." In some instances, I have quoted at length the letters and written recollections submitted to me, information which provides unique insights into the writers and their relationships to the composer.

In addition, in many instances, I have quoted Virgil Thomson's own recollections about his portrait subjects—information which is probably of more value to the readers of this catalog than general biographical data. The following symbols are used to indicate the source of the Thomson quotations:

(VT):   Excerpts from my interviews with Virgil Thomson held between January, 1982 and January, 1985.

(VT 1):   Thomson's own typed program notes. Many of these have appeared in the various published editions, but some have not. These typed notes come from Thomson's private documents. (All published editions of portraits which include program notes are listed in the bibliography.)

(VT 2):   Liner notes by Thomson for recordings of portraits (all of which are listed in the bibliography).

(VT 3):   Excerpts from Thomson's autobiography, *Virgil Thomson by Virgil Thomson* (New York: Alfred A. Knopf, 1966; E. P. Dutton, Inc., 1985), with page references.

6. SOURCES

With the exception of the portraits from 1981-1985, nearly all the original manuscripts for the Thomson portraits are located in the Virgil Thomson Collection at the Beinecke Rare Book and Manuscript Library at Yale University. For nearly every portrait located at the Beinecke Library I have listed after the word "Manuscript" two reference numbers:

1. The Box/Folder numbers for the Thomson Collection.
2. The call number (in parentheses) for the manuscript as listed in the original Cardell catalog for the Thomson Collection. For example:

   Manuscript - 10/2 (P26)

This means the manuscript is filed in the Thomson Collection in Box 10, Folder 2, with the Cardell listing P26.

For the 1981-1985 portraits (numbers 93 - 140), I have used the following abbreviation:

   Manuscript (Photocopy-Yale)

This indicates that Mr. Thomson possesses the manuscript but the Beinecke Library has a photocopy.

Following this information I have listed all the published editions, if any, in which each portrait appears, including editions of transcriptions where appropriate. As of this writing a majority of the portraits are now available in published editions. I have devised a system of abbreviated references to these editions. The abbreviations are as follows:

EIGHT PORTRAITS: *Eight Portraits: for Violin Alone*, edited with Bowings and Fingerings by Joseph Fuchs (New York: Boosey and Hawkes, 1981).

FIVE LADIES: *Five Ladies for Violin and Piano*, (New York: G. Schirmer, Inc., 1983).

PORTRAITS I: *Portraits for Piano Solo: Album One*, (New York: G. Schirmer, Inc., 1969). First published by Mercury Music Corp., New York, 1948.

PORTRAITS II: *Portraits for Piano Solo: Album Two*, (New York: G. Schirmer, Inc., 1969). First published by Mercury Music Corp., New York, 1949.

PORTRAITS III: *Portraits for Piano Solo: Album Three*, (New York: G. Schirmer, Inc., 1969). First published by Mercury Music Corp., New York, 1950.

PORTRAITS IV: *Portraits for Piano: Album Four*, (New York: G. Schirmer, Inc., 1969). First published by Mercury Music Corp., New York, 1953.

NINE PORTRAITS: *Nine Portraits for Piano*, (New York: Southern Music Publishing Company, 1974).

THIRTEEN PORTRAITS: *Thirteen Portraits: for Piano*, (New York: Boosey And Hawkes, 1981).

NINETEEN PORTRAITS: *Nineteen Portraits: for Piano (1981)*, (New York: Boosey and Hawkes, 1981).

*SEVENTEEN PORTRAITS: *Seventeen Portraits for Piano (1983-84)*, (New York: G. Schirmer, Inc., 1984).

* Due to be released in 1985.

All other miscellaneous editions of individual portraits, or collections of music containing portraits are fully listed in the body of the thematic catalog.

7. RECORDINGS

As of this writing there are seven recordings which contain Virgil Thomson portraits that are currently available. Spectrum Records has begun a project to record all of the Virgil Thomson piano music performed by Yvar Mikhashoff. To date, only one record from this series has been released.

The six recordings will be referred to in the catalog by the following abbreviations:

NS   *Virgil Thomson: A Portrait Album* (Nonesuch: New York, 1981) D-79024.

Contains:
Twelve Selected Portraits for Piano (Paul Jacobs, piano and harpsichord);
Eight Portraits for Violin Alone (Joseph Silverstein, violin);
Family Portrait (American Brass Quartet).

FINN   *Virgil Thomson: Piano Music,* performed by Arthur Tollefson (Finndar Records: New York, 1980)
SR 9027.
Contains:
Six Selected Portraits for Piano;
Ten Etudes; Nine Etudes.

CRI   *American Historic: Music of Virgil Thomson* (Composer Recordings Incorporated: New York, 1979).
Originally recorded by Columbia Records.
Contains:
Three Portraits, transcribed for orchestra —
Bugles and Birds, Tango Lullaby, Fugue; Philadelphia Orchestra, Virgil Thomson, conductor.
Also,
Three Pictures for Orchestra; Three Songs of William Blake.

SPEC *Hear America First Recording Project, Volume 4; Virgil Thomson: 60 Years of Piano Music* (Harrimon, New York: Spectrum-Division of Unipro, 1982). Yvar Mikhashoff, piano.
Contains:
Sixteen Piano Portraits from 1981;
"Suite" from *The Plow That Broke the Plains; Ten Easy Pieces and a Coda.*

MHS *Piano Music by Virgil Thomson* performed by Nigel Coxe (Musical Heritage Society: Ocean, NJ, 1983) MHS Stereo 4804T.
Contains:
Portraits, Album One (Complete)
Portraits, Album Three(Complete)
Piano Sonata No. 1
Piano Sonata No. 2

ETC   *American Piano Music,* Bennett Lerner, pianist. (Etcetera Records B.V.: Amsterdam, 1984) ETC 1091.
Contains:
Thomson, Two Portraits (1983)
Thomson, Two Sentimental Tangos, (1923); plus music by Copland, Bowles, Barber, Bernstein, and Ramey.

OSHKOSH *Music of Virgil Thomson: Premiere Recording of Eleven Portraits for Orchestra, and Acadian Songs and Dances* performed by Oshkosh Symphony Orchestra, Henri B. Pensis, conductor (Henri B. Pensis, producer).

Write to: The Oshkosh Symphony, Inc., P.O. Box 522, Oshkosh, Wisconsin 54902

Contains:

Eleven Portraits for Orchestra (1982)

Orchestrated by Rodney Lister:

Bill Katz: Wide Awake

Christopher Cox: Singing a Song

Sam Byers: With Joy

Orchestrated by Scott Wheeler:

Dennis Russell Davies: In a Hammock

Richard Flender: Solid Not Stolid

Scott Wheeler: Free Wheeling

Orchestrated by Virgil Thomson:

Loyal, Steady, Persistent: Noah Creshevsky

Intensely Two: Karen Brown Waltuck

A Love Scene (Anonymous) — transformation of *Dead Pan*

David Dubal: In Flight

Something of a Beauty: Anne-Marie Soulliére

Also,

Acadian Songs and Dances (1948)

A Chronological
List of Portraits

THE
THEMATIC
CATALOG

1. **Señorita Juanita de Medina accompanied by her mother**

DATE: 21 July, 1928; Ascain, France

SCORING: Violin solo

SUBJECT: A young Spanish woman who played the violin. She was staying at a hotel in Ascain where Thomson was vacationing. (For a detailed account of this subject and the composition of this portrait, see page 33, or VT 3, p. 123.)

SOURCES: Manuscript - 7/18 (P47A); *Eight Portraits*

RECORDINGS: NS

2.   Madame Marthe-Marthine

DATE: 31 August, 1928; Bagnoles-de-l'Orne, France

SCORING: Violin solo

SUBJECT: Wife of composer-pianist Henri Cliquet-Pleyel.
(VT 3, p. 109) - "Madame Marthe-Marthine was plumpish, blond, the classical sou-
brette, alert and sex-minded, also a singer of remarkable musicianship."

SOURCES: Manuscript - 7/18 (P44); *Eight Portraits*

RECORDINGS: NS

3.   Georges Hugnet: Poet and Man of Letters

DATE: October, 1928; Paris. Chronological placement as no. 3 determined by Thomson's
personal recollection.

SCORING: Violin solo

SUBJECT: Georges Hugnet (b. Paris, 1906); French surrealist poet, editor, art critic, and essay-
ist. Hugnet's essays are collected in *Fantastic Art, Dada, Surrealism*, edited by Alfred
Barr, Jr., essays by Georges Hugnet (New York: Museum of Modern Art, 1968).
Hugnet is a recurring figure in Thomson's autobiography (see VT 3, p. 94, for a
lengthy description). Also the subject of portrait no. 45.

SOURCES: Manuscript - 7/18 (P30B); *Eight Portraits*

RECORDINGS: NS

Georges Hugnet, 1927; photo by
Man Ray, copyright Juliet Man Ray,
1985. (From the collection of Virgil
Thomson.)

4.   Cliquet-Pleyel in F

DATE: 14 October, 1928; Paris
            Written same day as no. 5. Chronological placement determined by Thomson's
            recollection.

SCORING: Violin solo

SUBJECT: Henri Cliquet-Pleyel (b. Paris, 1894; d. Paris, 1963); French composer. Studied with
            Koechlin at the Paris Conservatoire. Active in Paris between the wars.
            (VT 1) - "French composer of the Ecole d'Arceuil (four composers including also
            Roger Désormière, Maxime Jacob, and Henri Sauguet), first presented as a group by
            Erik Satie in 1924 at the Collège de France." (For a description of Cliquet-Pleyel, see
            VT 3, p. 109.)

SOURCES: Manuscript - 7/18 (P18.2); *Eight Portraits*

RECORDINGS: NS

5. Miss Gertrude Stein As A Young Girl

DATE: 14 October, 1928; Paris

SCORING: Violin solo

SUBJECT: Gertrude Stein (b. Allegheny, Pennsylvania, 1872; d. Paris, 1946); American-born, Paris-based writer.
(VT 1) - "Gertrude Stein, known to the composer 'as a young girl' only through her writings. She was fifty-two when Thomson met her." One of the most important of Thomson's collaborators, Stein appears as a major figure in his autobiography. (See VT 3).

SOURCES: Manuscript - 7/18 (P61.5); *Eight Portraits*

RECORDINGS: NS

Gertrude Stein and Alice B. Toklas in the middle 1920s; from the collection of Virgil Thomson.

6.   Mrs. Chester Whitin Lasell

DATE: 18 October, 1928; Paris

SCORING: Violin solo

SUBJECT: Jessie K. (Mrs. Chester Whitin) Lasell. Born in San Francisco (Jessie Keeler). In 1886, married Chester Whitin Lasell, a manufacturer of textile machinery, resident in Whitinsville, Massachusetts. Became Thomson's patron in 1927 after he arranged for a doctor to treat her when she fell ill in Normandy. Mrs. Lasell is a recurring figure in Thomson's autobiography. (See VT 3, pp. 74, 99, 127-130, 352.) Also the subject of Thomson portrait no. 69.

SOURCES: Manuscript - 7/18 (P38A); *Eight Portraits*

RECORDINGS: NS

Jessie K. Lasell c. 1930; from the collection of Virgil Thomson.

7.   Sauguet: From Life

DATE: 5 November, 1928; Paris

SCORING: Violin solo

SUBJECT: Henri Sauguet, French composer, (b. Bordeaux, 1901). Protègé of Erik Satie. Wrote
           operas, ballets, symphonies, vocal music. Bibliography: M. Schneider, *Henri Sauguet*
           (Paris, 1959).

           (VT 1) - "A composer of the Group d'Arceuil and a member of the Institut de
           France."

Henri Sauguet; from the collection of
Virgil Thomson.

SOURCES:
Manuscript - 7/18 (P57); *Eight Portraits*
RECORDINGS: NS

Five Portraits for Four Clarinets: (8-12)

8.   Portrait of Ladies: A Conversation

DATE: 16 January, 1929; Kansas City

SCORING: Two B-flat clarinets, E-flat alto clarinet (originally basset horn), B-flat bass clarinet

SUBJECT: (VT 1) - " 'Portrait of Ladies' represents four women of my acquaintance who had so long and so cheerfully lived together that they could all talk at the same time without interference. They could tell a story as a quartet of instruments might, handing the theme of it back and forth almost in counterpoint."

(VT) - "They were three sisters and one cousin, descendents of Peter Stuyvestant. The sisters were Mrs. Dwight Braman, Fanny Dudley, and Laura Dudley. The cousin was Miss Julia Winterhoff."

SOURCES: Manuscript - 7/11 (P35.5); *Five Portraits for Four Clarinets* (New York: G. Schirmer, 1977).

9. Christian Bérard: Prisonnier

DATE: 4 & 8 May, 1929; Paris

SCORING: Two A clarinets, E-flat alto clarinet (originally basset horn), B-flat bass clarinet

SUBJECT.   Christian Bérard (1902-1949), French painter, decorator, stage designer. (VT) - "This is a portrait of the artist at work, painting my portrait as I wrote his. Bérard lived in a ground-level house in Paris that had bars on the windows. So when you sat inside you felt you were in a prison." (Also subject of portraits 11 and 12.)

SOURCES: Manuscript - 7/11 (P9.51); *Five Portraits for Four Clarinets* (New York: G. Schirmer, 1977)

Christian Bérard in Paris, c. 1927; from the collection of Virgil Thomson.

10.   Portrait of a Young Man in Good Health

DATE: 7 July, 1929; Villefranche-sur-mer

SCORING: Two A clarinets, E-flat clarinet (originally basset horn), B-flat bass clarinet

SUBJECT: Maurice Grosser (b. Huntsville, Alabama, 1903). Painter and author. Provided sce-
            narios for *Four Saints in Three Acts* and *The Mother of Us All. Books by Grosser include:*
            The Painter's Eye (New York: Rinehart, 1951) and *Painting in Public* (New York:
            Knopf, 1948).
            (VT 1) - "Maurice posed for me one day while immobilized by a huge cold in the
            head. It was the contrast of this temporary symptom with his basic energies that
            caused me to call my piece *Portrait of a Young Man in Good Health.*" (Also subject of
            Thomson portrait no. 14.)

SOURCES: Manuscript - 7/11 (P26D); *Five Portraits for Four Clarinets* (New York: G. Schirmer,
            1977)

Maurice Grosser, 1934, by Lee Miller;
from the collection of Virgil
Thomson.

11.   "Bébé" Soldat

(Cl. 1 & 2)

DATE: 9 July, 1929; Villefranche-sur-mer

SCORING: Two A clarinets, E-flat alto clarinet (originally basset horn), B-flat bass clarinet

SUBJECT: Christian Bérard (See portrait no. 9)
           (VT 1) - "This portrait, a bit of comic relief, shows him during the 28 days of military
           service demanded of every French soldier five years after release from his original
           call-up. 'Bébé' was his French nickname."

SOURCES: Manuscript - 7/11 (P9.50); *Five Portraits for Four Clarinets*, (New York: G. Schirmer,
           1977)

12.   Christian Bérard in Person

DATE: 11 July, 1929; Villefranche-sur-mer

SCORING: Two B-flat clarinets, E-flat alto clarinet (originally basset horn), B-flat bass clarinet

SUBJECT: Christian Bérard (See portrait no. 9)
           (VT 1) - "This portrait attempts to give the feeling of his actual presence, which was
           one of intelligence and gaiety, both qualities exaggerated in him almost to the point
           of self-indulgence."

SOURCES: Manuscript - 7/11 (P9.52); *Five Portraits for Four Clarinets* (New York: G. Schirmer,
           1977)

13.   Travelling in Spain: Alice Woodfin Branlière

DATE: 24 October, 1929; Paris

SCORING: Piano

SUBJECT: (VT 1) - "Alice Woodfin Branlière was an American lady from Vermont, a musician and a friend, long resident in Paris."

SOURCES: Manuscript - 10/7 (P13); *Thirteen Portraits*

Alice Woodfin Branlière; from the collection of Virgil Thomson.

14.   Alternations: A Portrait of Maurice Grosser

DATE: 28 October, 1929; Paris

SCORING: Piano

SUBJECT: Maurice Grosser (See portrait no. 10. Also, see chapter V for an analysis of this portrait.)

SOURCES: Manuscript - 10/2 (P26A); *Portraits I*

RECORDINGS: NS; FINN; MHS

15.   Catalan Waltz: A Portrait of Ramon Senabre

DATE: 2 November, 1929; La Grange-Bleneau

SCORING: Piano

SUBJECT: (VT) - "Ramon Senabre is a Catalonian painter who lived in Paris—he came from Barcelona—and whom I've known for forty or fifty years. He's older than I am but last year I knew he was still extant."

SOURCES: Manuscript - 10/3 (P59); *Portraits II*

RECORDINGS: NS; FINN

Ramon Senabre, 1931; from the
collection of Virgil Thomson.

16.   Clair Leonard's Profile

DATE: 22 January, 1930; Paris

SCORING: Piano

SUBJECT: Clair Leonard, American composer (b. Newton, MA 1901; d. 1963). Graduated
            from Harvard in the early 1920s, received Naumburg and Paine fellowships. Studied
            in Paris with Nadia Boulanger. Taught briefly at Harvard, also at Wellesley, Vassar,
            and Bard. Wrote orchestral, chamber, choral music, and several stage works, includ-
            ing music for *My Country Right or Left* and *Dance of Death*, both produced in 1935 at
            Vassar Theatre and Adelphi Theatre, New York.

SOURCES: Manuscript - 10/6 (P39A); *Thirteen Portraits*

17.   Madame Dubost chez elle

DATE: 1 February, 1930; Paris

SCORING: Piano; arranged for solo trombone with viola and cello accompaniment by Yvar
            Mikhashoff (unpublished)

SUBJECT: (VT) - "Madame Dubost was a sweet French lady and a musical hostess. She was
            kind to musicians and many went to her house. At one time the composers she had
            been kind to and friendly with all made her a little gift, a festschrift in the form of a
            fan. I was not amongst those but I later did this portrait for myself, a little picture, a
            sketch of her at her own house. I remember this as not made in person, from life."

SOURCES: Manuscript - 10/6 (P23); *Nine Portraits*

18.   Pastorale: A Portrait of Jean Ozenne

DATE: 20 February, 1930; Paris

SCORING: Piano

SUBJECT: (VT) - "Jean Ozenne was a cousin of the painter Christian Bérard. Jean spent many
            years of his life as a dress designer. But in his last fifteen or twenty years he was an
            actor in good plays and had small roles in cinema. Along with Bérard and Sauguet,
            he was an old friend of Christian Dior. He came from the French upper-middle class.
            He was about my age, died of cancer around 1960."

SOURCES: Manuscript (P51); *Portraits III*

RECORDINGS: MHS

19.   Alice Toklas

DATE: 24 March, 1930; Paris

SCORING: Violin and piano

SUBJECT: Alice Toklas (b. San Francisco, 1877; d. Paris, 1967). Author and companion of
            Gertrude Stein. For an account of her life, see Gertrude Stein, *The Autobiography of
            Alice B. Toklas*, published in *Selected Writings of Gertrude Stein*, ed. Carl Van Vechten
            (New York: Random House, 1946), and Alice B. Toklas, *What is Remembered* (New
            York: Holt, Rinehart & Winston, 1963).

SOURCES: Manuscript - 7/18 (P65.5); *Five Ladies*

Alice B. Toklas, Gertrude Stein, and
Harold MacCormick, November
1934, *Four Saints* Chicago premiere,
Auditorium Theatre; from the
collection of Virgil Thomson.

20. Mary Reynolds

DATE: 15 April, 1930; Villefranche-sur-mer

SCORING: Violin and Piano

SUBJECT: Mary Reynolds, American war-widow from Minneapolis. Collector of art and books. Skilled bookbinder.
(VT 1) - "From Minneapolis, friend of artists, and a bookbinder, inveterately Parisian. To avoid wartime arrest she walked over the Pyrenees."
(VT 3, p. 204) - "Mary Reynolds received modest sustenance from a well-off but grudging father who considered sinful her gracious way of life."

SOURCES: Manuscript 7/18 (P54); *Five Ladies*

Mary Reynolds, 1930; photo by Man Ray, copyright Juliet Man Ray, 1985. (From the collection of Virgil Thomson.)

21.   Anne Miracle

DATE: 21 April, 1930; Villefranche-sur-mer

SCORING: Violin and piano

SUBJECT: (VT 1) - "Anne Miracle. French, beauteous, and sweet."
            (VT) - "Anne Miracle was the first wife of Ralph Mannheim, who is a principal
            translator of German books these days. Ralph Mannheim himself was the first hus-
            band of Sylvia Marlowe [the late American harpsichordist]. But his first wife was this
            little French girl Anne Miracle, although if that was her real name we never knew.
            She was also at one point a kind of girlfriend to Paul Bowles."

SOURCES: Manuscript - 7/18 (P47.5); *Five Ladies*

22.   **Russell Hitchcock, Reading**

DATE: 29 May, 1930; Paris

SCORING: Piano; arranged for solo trombone with viola and cello accompaniment by Yvar
            Mikhashoff (unpublished)

SUBJECT: Henry-Russell Hitchcock (b. Boston, 1903); noted historian of architecture and art
            critic. Studied at Harvard; taught at Wesleyan, Smith, New York University. Helped
            organize and sponsor the first production of *Four Saints* in Hartford, Connecticut.
            (VT) - "Well, I've known Russell for sixty years or more. Russell is, I suppose, the
            most famous architectural historian in the world. He's over eighty now and not at all
            well. But he's still a close friend. His portrait was made in the early days when he

Henry-Russell Hitchcock, ca. 1939;
photo by George Platt Lynes,
American, 1907-1955; Collection,
Vassar College Art Gallery,
Poughkeepsie, NY; Gift of Agnes
Rindge Claflin.

used to spend, as a young man and a student, winters in Paris learning things about
architecture, also traveling. But he always had a little hotel room very near to where
I lived and we would very often have lunch together and then go for a walk. I'd walk
all over Paris with Russell and he'd explain to me how to read the architecture. After
two years I knew practically all of it."

SOURCES: Manuscript - 10/7 (P29); *Nine Portraits*

23.   **Sea Coast: A Portrait of Constance Askew**

DATE: 30 April, 1935; New York

SCORING: Piano

SUBJECT: Constance Askew (b. 1895; d. 1984), wife of R. Kirk Askew, the New York art dealer (see portrait no. 24). Married in 1929. An important hostess and patron to artists and writers. (For a detailed portrait of Constance and Kirk Askew see VT 3, pp. 215-216.)

(VT) - "Constance Askew was a New England woman. Her family name was Atwood. They were extremely well-to-do. Her father and, I presume, grandfather owned a factory for making silk-weaving machinery in Stonington, Connecticut. Kirk Askew was her second husband. The title "Sea Coast" has to do with her, being a strikingly beautiful woman but kind of rock-bound. Constance was about two years older than I. For the last years of her life, she lived in New York, immobilized, with nurses 'round the clock. She never went out, or at least very rarely. But she had visitors and three daughters, one by Walter Macoomb (her first husband) and two by Askew. Macoomb's daughter, Pamela Askew, is a professor of art history at Vassar."

SOURCES: Manuscript - 10/7 (P50); *Portraits II*

Mrs. R. Kirk Askew, Jr., ca. 1930s;
courtesy of Professor Pamela Askew.

24.   A Portrait of R. Kirk Askew, Jr.

(L.H. tacet) **mp** semplice

DATE: 1 May, 1935; New York

SCORING: Piano

SUBJECT: R. Kirk Askew (b. Kansas City, 1903; d. 1974), American art dealer. Studied at M.I.T. and Harvard. Became director both in New York and London of Durlacher Brothers Gallery (Bond Street, London) and, in 1937, an owner as well. Married Constance Atwood Macoomb (see portrait no. 23) in 1929.
          (VT 3, p. 214) - "Kirk Askew was slight of frame with curvaceous facial forms that gave him a carved-in-mahogany aspect which accorded well with his Victorian house."

SOURCES: Manuscript - 10/6 (P6); *Portraits II*

R. Kirk Askew, Jr., ca. 1930s (photo by Carl van Vechter); courtesy of Professor Pamela Askew.

25. An Old Song: A Portrait of Carrie Stettheimer

DATE: 5 May, 1935; New York
Written the same day as no.26. Chronological placement determined by Thomson's recollection.

SCORING: Piano

SUBJECT: Carrie Walter Stettheimer (d. 1944); sister of artist Florine Stettheimer (see portrait no. 71) and the writer Ettie Stettheimer (see portrait no. 26).

(VT) - "Carrie Stettheimer spent twenty years making the famous dollhouse now at the Museum of the City of New York. The title, "An Old Song," has nothing to do with the doll's house, except that the same quality in her that made her build the doll's house was the quality that I interpreted as a nicely sentimental old song. Of the three sisters, when they all lived together surrounding an invalid mother, it was Carrie who did most of the housekeeping. Oh, they had servants who really did it, but I mean to order the meals and see to everything."

The construction and contents of the Carrie Stettheimer dollhouse are described in an illustrated book by John Noble, Curator of the Toy Collection at the Museum of the City of New York, *A Fabulous Dollhouse of the Twenties* (New York: Dover, 1976). One room, an art gallery, contains miniature works made especially for this dollhouse by several important artists, including Marcel Duchamp, Gaston Lachaise, and Gela Archipenko.

SOURCES: Manuscript (P62); *Portraits I*

RECORDINGS: NS; MHS

26.   Ettie Stettheimer

DATE: 5 May, 1935; New York

SCORING: Piano; arranged for solo trombone with viola and cello accompaniment by Yvar
           Mikhashoff (unpublished)

SUBJECT: Ettie Stettheimer (d. 1950), the youngest of the three Stettheimer sisters (See por-
           traits no. 25, and 71). An author with a Ph.D. from the University of Freiburg.
           Published two novels under the pseudonym Henry Waste.

SOURCES: Manuscript - 10/4 (P62.5); *Nine Portraits*

27.   Tennis: A Portrait of Henry McBride

DATE: 9 May, 1935; New York

SCORING: Piano

SUBJECT: Henry McBride (b. West Chester, Pennsylvania 1867; d. 1962.) Art reviewer and
           critic for *The Dial*, and, for thirty-six years, *The New York Sun*. Reported on the first
           production of *Four Saints*. A supporter and friend of Gertrude Stein.
           His writings have been collected in *Essays and Criticisms of Henry McBride*; selected,
           with an Introduction by Daniel Catton Rich (New York: Athenaeum Publishers,
           1975). In the "Quasi-Preface" to this collection, Lincoln Kirstein describes McBride's
           experience posing for Thomson's portrait. From Kirstein's account I quote the fol-
           lowing (p. 15):

When McBride went to pose, in the ample salon at Mrs. Kirk Askew's in the East Sixties (in the mid Thirties), Thomson placed him in a comfortable chair. McBride took a book, commenced to read, silently. 'Perhaps Virgil would like to have been interrupted, but I didn't.' At the end of the portrait there is a brilliant tennis game, perhaps a reference to the Seabright matches in the Stettheimer picture. When McBride was played the portrait, which enchanted him, he said: 'Evidently, I won the game.' Replied the composer, 'You certainly did.'

(VT) - "Henry McBride was a prominent art critic and his work is collected now. He was a tennis player. Oh yes, so I made a tennis game. You bat that ball forward and smash it and do all the tennis things in there."

SOURCES: Manuscript - 10/7 (P46A); *Portraits IV*

---

28.   **Philip Claflin: dans le temps très noceur**

DATE: May, 1935 and 14 March, 1985
Specific date of 1935 composition not known. Chronological placement determined by Virgil Thomson's recollection.

SCORING: Piano

SUBJECT: Philip W. Claflin (b. Quincy, Massachusetts 1904). Worked in the securities business on Wall Street for forty years. Educated at Exeter Academy and Harvard, where he studied architecture. Married Agnes Millicent Rindge (portrait no. 33) in 1944. Since 1968 has lived in retirement on a farm in New Paltz, New York.

SOURCES: Manuscript (photocopy-Yale)

29.   Souvenir: A Portrait of Paul Bowles

DATE: 20 May, 1935; New York

SCORING: Piano

SUBJECT: Paul Bowles (b. New York, 1910); author and composer. Studied with Copland and Virgil Thomson. His work has been influenced by his extensive visits to Morocco and Central America and his research into the folklore of these regions. A composer of chamber music, theatre music, songs, and an opera *The Wind Remains* (libretto by Federico García Lorca). A fiction writer of international acclaim. His wife, the late Jane Bowles (1917-73) is considered by many scholars to be a major American author. (See portrait no. 79.) Paul Bowles has written an autobiography, *Without Stopping* (New York: Putnam, 1972).

(VT) - "Paul Bowles was a composer. He later became quite a famous novelist. [The title "Souvenir?"] Well, I've known Paul for a long time and maybe that's what it is. And Janie? Oh yes, I think I may have introduced them. But we all knew Jane that first year she appeared amongst us like a miracle. She was 18 or 16, very young. It was a strange and elaborate marriage, but they were very devoted to each other."

SOURCES: Manuscript - 10/7 (P12); *Portraits III*

RECORDINGS: MHS

Paul Bowles, 1951; courtesy of Mr. Paul Bowles.

30.   The Hunt: A Portrait of A. E. Austin, Jr.

DATE: 21 May, 1935; New York

SCORING: Piano

SUBJECT: A. Everett ("Chick") Austin, Jr. (b. Brookline, MA 1900; d. Hartford, 1957), director
            of the Wadsworth Athenaeum in Hartford, Connecticut from 1927-1944. He cham-
            pioned the addition of film, opera, concerts, and dance to the activities of American
            museums. Built the Athenaeum's modern wing, equipped with a theatre, the site of
            the first production of *Four Saints*.
            (VT 3, p. 207) - "Chick was a man of substance, young, my own classmate, an
            entrepreneur of unrestrained imagination."
            (VT) - "He was a very advanced picture buyer among museum directors. He brought

A. Everett Austin, 1934; from the
collection of Virgil Thomson.

to attention and launched the collecting of Baroque painting. [Regarding the portrait's title?] Chick was a hunter of people as well as of pictures, and thoroughly cheerful about it all."

SOURCES: Manuscript - 10/5 (P7); *Portraits IV*

---

31.   Hymn: A Portrait of Josiah Marvel

DATE: 22 May, 1935; New York

SCORING: Piano

SUBJECT: Josiah Marvel (b. 1896; d. Reading, Vermont 1959). Born to a Quaker family in Pennsylvania. First director of the Springfield Museum of Fine Arts, founded in 1934. Was the director of the American Friends Service Committee in France at the start of World War II.

SOURCES: Manuscript - 10/5 (P45); *Portraits IV*

---

32.   The John Mosher Waltzes

DATE: May, 1935; New York
                Specific date of composition unknown. Chronological placement determined by Thomson's recollection.

SCORING: Piano; included as part of Thomson's ballet *Filling Station* - No. 6, "Family Life," 1937
             (Orchestration: piano, harp, timpani, percussion, strings)

SUBJECT: John Chapin Mosher (b. Albany, 1892; d. New York, 1942). Joined the staff of *The
             New Yorker* in 1926; was their film critic from 1926 until his death.
             (VT) - "John Mosher was a film critic for *The New Yorker* magazine for twenty or
             more years. Also the author of a book of short stories. He was on the staff there from
             almost the very beginning."

SOURCES: Manuscript - 10/5 (P48); *Filling Station, arr. for piano-two hands, by Virgil Thomson
             (New York: Arrow Music Press, 1942); later published by Boosey & Hawkes.*

---

33.   **Prelude and Fugue: A Portrait of Miss Agnes Rindge**

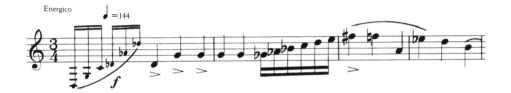

Agnes Rindge, 1939, photo by
GEORGE PLATT LYNES;
Collection, Vassar College Art
Gallery, Poughkeepsie, NY; Gift of
Leila Cook Barber.

DATE: 2 September, 1935; Castine, Maine

SCORING: Piano

SUBJECT: Agnes Millicent Rindge (b. Grand Rapids, Michigan 1900; d. New Paltz, NY 1978).
           Attended Radcliffe, received A.B., M.A., and Ph.D in art history. Awarded the
           Radcliffe Medal (to distinguished alumni) in 1950. Taught at Vassar College, chair-
           man of the art department for nearly forty years. Hired Alfred Barr, Jr. (his first job),
           and A. Everett Austin, Jr.
           Author of *Sculpture* (New York: Payson & Clarke, Ltd., 1929). Married Philip W.
           Claflin (portrait no 28) in 1944

SOURCES: Manuscript - 10/6 (P55A); *Portraits III*

RECORDINGS: MHS

---

34.   Helen Austin at Home and Abroad

DATE: 3 September, 1935; Bangor, Maine

SCORING: Piano

SUBJECT: "Helen Austin, granddaughter of the Rev. Francis Goodwin and a cousin of Mu-
           seum of Modern Art architect Philip L. Goodwin, married A. Everett Austin, Jr. in
           1929. She has been a gracious presence in Hartford all her life." - Program Notes,
           Hartford Symphony Orchestra Anniversary Concert, May 12, 1984; Wadsworth
           Athenaeum, Hartford, Connecticut. (See portrait no. 30, A. Everett Austin, Jr.)

SOURCES: Manuscript - 10/5 (P8A); *Nine Portraits*

Mrs. A. Everett Austin, Jr., c. 1930s;
courtesy of Sarah Goodwin Austin.

35.   Meditation: A Portrait of Jere Abbott

DATE: 6 September, 1935; Castine, Maine

SCORING: Piano; arr. for orchestra in 1944 by Virgil Thomson

SUBJECT: Jere Abbott (b. 1897; d. 1982), art scholar, museum director, executive. Studied
physics at Bowdoin and Harvard, and art history at Princeton. Was the Associate
Director of the Museum of Modern Art in New York at the time of its founding
(1929), and during the early tenure of Alfred Barr, Jr., a college friend. Left that

position in 1932 to become a professor at Smith College and the director of the Smith College Museum of Art. Became treasurer of his family business, the Abbott Woolen Manufacturing Company, after his retirement from teaching.

SOURCES: Manuscript, piano version - 10/6 (P1); *Portraits II; Manuscript, orchestral version:* "Meditation" (P1A)

---

36. Connecticut Waltz: Harold Lewis Cook

DATE: 16 September, 1935; Avon Old Farms, Connecticut

SCORING: Piano

SUBJECT: (VT) - "Harold Cook was a poet and an instructor at a boys school in Connecticut called Avon Old Farms. He had been to Cambridge University in England. It was he who had proposed I do this portrait. In fact, he commissioned it. I've occasionally had letters from him. He lives in Mexico now and has become an Episcopal clergyman."

SOURCES: Manuscript - 10/3 (P18.5); *Thirteen Portraits*

---

37. A Day Dream: A Portrait of Herbert Whiting

DATE: 17 September, 1935; Avon Old Farms, Connecticut

SCORING: Piano

SUBJECT: (VT) - "Herbert Whiting was a young man with some literary gifts and an instructor at a boy's school in Connecticut called Avon Old Farms. He was a colleague there and friend of Harold Lewis Cook [portrait no. 36]."

SOURCES: Manuscript - 10/3 (P70A); *A Day Dream: Portrait of Herbert Whiting* (New York: Carl Fischer, 1941 - Archive Edition)

---

38. Portrait of Claude Biais

(L.H. tacet)

DATE: 15 August, 1938; Lamoura, France

SCORING: Piano

SUBJECT: Three young French boys were staying at a hotel in Lamoura, France where Thomson was vacationing during August, 1938. Thomson sketched their portraits on three successive days—Claude Biais (no. 38), Louis Lange (no. 39), and Maurice Bavoux (no. 40).

(VT) - "Claude Biais was a child of ten or so. He was very simple and straightforward, if children ever are straightforward. Nice, plain kid. A French boy staying with his family in a hotel at a village called Lamoura in the Jura mountains."

SOURCES: Manuscript - 10/3 (P10)

---

39. A French Boy of Ten: Louis Lange

DATE: 16 August, 1938; Lamoura, France

SCORING: Piano

SUBJECT: (VT) - "Louis Lange was a young French boy. As a child in the country, he was staying at the same hotel and I got him to pose for me. He was about ten. That was before the war. After the war I had a letter from him. He had grown up, heard that I still existed, so I gave him a copy of his portrait. He wrote to tell me who he still was."

SOURCES: Manuscript - 10/4 (P37); *Nine Portraits*

---

40.   Maurice Bavoux: Young and Alone

DATE: 17 and 18 August, 1938; Lamoura, France

SCORING: Piano

SUBJECT: Letter from Maurice Bavoux to the author, dated 30 September, 1984:

> I made Mr. Virgil Thomson's acquaintance while he was staying in the French village of Lamoura (Jura district) in the summer of 1938; I was then 19 years old. I was actually born in this village, a small resort for summer and winter holidays, nicely situated at an altitude of 1,150 meters.
>
> In those days, Mr. Thomson was accompanied by a friend of his, Mr. Maurice Grosser, a painter. As I agreed to sit for Mr. Grosser, Mr. Thomson composed my portrait by way of thanks and gave me a copy of it which is still in my possession. Many years later, in 1972, I wrote to Mr. Thomson again and he sent me a photograph of the painted portrait that Mr. Grosser had made of me. In my opinion, the painted portrait should be the ideal companion piece to the musical portrait, as they were made almost simultaneously, the latter being the consequence of the former.
>
> I started my career as a customs officer in 1939 and retired in May, 1983. I spent most of my professional duty in the Lorraine area and have lived in Metz since 1950. I got married in 1943. My elder daughter, a math teacher, has spent every summer in the USA for the last ten years, acting as a chaperon for young French students staying with American families. My younger daughter and her husband (who translated this letter for me) both teach English."

SOURCES: Manuscript - 10/6 (P9.2); *Thirteen Portraits*

Maurice Bavoux, 1938, painting by Maurice Grosser; courtesy of Maurice Grosser.

Maurice Bavoux, 1970s; courtesy of Maurice Bavoux.

41.   The Bard: Portrait of Sherry Mangan

DATE: 1 April, 1940; Paris

SCORING: Piano

SUBJECT: John Joseph Sherry Mangan (b. Lynn, MA 1904; d. Rome, 1961), magazine editor, novelist, poet, short-story writer, book designer. Internationally renowned journalist during World War II, for *Time*, *Life*, and *Fortune*. A dedicated Marxist, later Trotsky-ist.
See Alan M. Wald, *The Revolutionary Imagination: The Poetry and Politics of John Wheelwright and Sherry Mangan* (Chapel Hill, 1983).
(VT) - "Sherry Mangan, an old friend of mine from college days, had become an addict of Trotskyist dogma and started working for the party, which he did for all the rest of his life along with another friend from Boston, a poet named John Wheel-wright. Jack was run down by a taxi cab on Commonwealth Avenue in front of his

Sherry Mangan, 1927; from the
collection of Virgil Thomson

own house but Sherry survived until about 1960 on various continents, editing and seeing through the press a Trotskyist paper in various languages. He was a classical scholar and a fine linguist. He wrote and published a number of books, poetry and fiction, and there is also an unpublished novel about tin miners in Bolivia."

SOURCES: Manuscript - 10/2 (P42A); *Portraits III*
RECORDINGS: MHS

42.   In a Bird Cage: A Portrait of Lise Deharme

DATE: 8 April, 1940; Paris

SCORING: Piano; transcribed for cello and piano in 1942 by Luigi Silva; transcribed for violin solo in 1947 by Samuel Dushkin; arranged for solo cello in 1982 by Frances-Marie Vitti

SUBJECT: (VT) - "Lise Deharme was a French woman poet who lived in a handsome Paris flat on the Place des Invalides. Her drawing room was a bird cage with birds actually flying around in it."

SOURCES: Manuscript - 10/5 (P22A); *Portraits II*; *Three Portraits for Violin and Piano*, transcribed by Samuel Dushkin (New York: G. Schirmer, 1947); *Four Portraits for Cello and Piano*, arranged by Luigi Silva (New York: G. Schirmer, 1979).

RECORDINGS: NS, FINN

43. With Trumpet and Horn: A Portrait of Louise Ardant

DATE: 11 April, 1940; Paris

SCORING: Piano

SUBJECT: (VT) - "Louise Ardant was a handsome young woman whose name suited her per-
           fectly. I didn't know her very well, but I asked her to pose one day and she did and
           that's what turned up."

SOURCES: Manuscript - 9/10 (P3A); published with title "With Trumpet and Horn" in *Nine
           Etudes for Piano* (New York: Carl Fischer, 1954), currently unavailable.

RECORDINGS: FINN

44. Poltergeist: A Portrait of Hans Arp

DATE: 12 April, 1940; Paris

SCORING: Piano

SUBJECT: Hans (or Jean) Arp, (1887-1966). Sculptor, painter, and poet. Born in Strasbourg,
           studied there and in Weimar and Paris (1909). Founder, along with Tristan Tzara (see
           portrait no. 57), of the Dada movement. Pioneer of abstract art and surrealism.
           Married in 1921 the Swiss abstractionist painter Sophie Taüber (see portrait no. 48).
           Bibliography: Herbert Read, *The Art of Jean Arp* (New York, 1968).
           (VT) - "Hans Arp. Later he called himself Jean Arp. But he was Alsatian by birth,
           an abstract sculptor. He came out as a sort of 'Poltergeist'."

SOURCES: Manuscript - 10/6 (P4A); *Portraits IV*

45.   Fanfare for France: A Portrait of Max Kahn

DATE: 15 April, 1940; Paris

SCORING: Piano; arranged for orchestra (brass and percussion) in 1944 by Virgil Thomson;
transcribed for cello and piano in 1942 by Luigi Silva.

SUBJECT: (VT) - "Max Kahn was an American who changed his name to Max Kenna. He
lived in Paris sharing a flat for many years with Jean Ozenne [see portrait no. 18]. He
went to the Parson's School of Design there and became a dress designer. I think it
was from Max that Jean learned to do that. Another friend of his was Christian
Dior, to whom he taught the technique."

SOURCES: Manuscript - 10/4 (P34); *Portraits II, Fanfare for France: Max Kahn*, for brass and
percussion (New York: Boosey & Hawkes, 1944); *Four Portraits for Cello and Piano*,
arranged by Luigi Silva (New York: G. Schirmer, 1979).

46.   Barcarolle: A Portrait of Georges Hugnet

DATE: 17 April, 1940; Paris
Composed same day as portrait no. 47. Chronological placement determined by
Thomson's recollection.

SCORING: Piano; arranged for woodwind orchestra in 1944 by Virgil Thomson; transcribed for
violin and piano in 1947 by Samuel Dushkin.

SUBJECT: Georges Hugnet (See portrait no. 3.)

SOURCES: Manuscript - 10/2 (P30); *Portraits I; Barcarolle for Woodwinds* (New York: G. Schirmer,
1944); *Three Portraits for Violin and Piano*, arranged by Samuel Dushkin (New York:
G. Schirmer, 1949).

RECORDINGS: NS; MHS

47.   Yvonne de Casa Fuerte

DATE: 17 April, 1940; Paris

SCORING: Violin and Piano

SUBJECT: Yvonne Giraud Alvarez de Toledo, Marquesa de Casa Fuerte (VT 1) - "Violinist,
Provençale by birth, married to a Spaniard, Franco-American by long musical experience."
(VT) - "A French violinist. Yvonne Giraud was her professional name. She married
a Spanish 'grandee' named Illan Alvarez de Toledo, Marquis de Casa Fuerte. He had

"La Sérénade," 1932 - (l. to r.)
Vittorio Rieti, Marqués de Casa
Fuerte, Milhaud, Prince Leone
Massimo, Yvonne de Casa Fuerte,
Sauguet, Désormière, and Igor
Markevitch; from the collection of
Virgil Thomson.

always lived in Italy because Phillip II had made one of the Marquis' great grandfathers a military governor in Naples. So the Casa Fuertes still lived in Italy but remained subject to the Spanish kings. Anyway, he married Yvonne. A great love affair. They had two children, a son and a daughter. Actually they had three but one died. Flavie, the daughter [see portrait no. 50], and a son Jean, who has been an extraordinary success in the shipping business in Argentina. After his father's death he provided generously for his mother and sister."

SOURCES: Manuscript (P17); *Five Ladies*

---

48.   Swiss Waltz: A Portrait of Sophie Taüber-Arp

DATE: 18 April, 1940; Paris

SCORING: Piano

SUBJECT: Sophie Henriette Taüber Arp (1889-1943); artist, sculptor. Swiss-born, studied at Saint Gall, Munich, Hamburg; taught textile design at Zürich School of Industrial Arts. Associated with Dada movement and Abstract Art. Made mechanical puppets, abstract sculptures, geometric paintings, abstract textiles. Founded the magazine *Plastique*. Married sculptor Hans Arp in 1921 (see portrait no. 44). Reference: Harris, A. S. and Nochlin, L., *Women Artists, 1550-1950* (New York: Knopf, 1976).

SOURCES: Manuscript - 10/7 (P64A); *Portraits IV*

---

49.   Eccentric Dance: Portrait of Madame Kristians Tonny

DATE: 20 April, 1940; Paris

SCORING: Piano

SUBJECT: Marie-Clair Ivanoff (Madame Kristians Tonny).
           Wife of the Dutch painter Kristians Tonny, né Anton Kristians (b. 1906).

SOURCES: Manuscript - 10/4 (P66A); *Eccentric Dance: Portrait of Madame Kristians Tonny* (New
           York: Carl Fisher, 1941; Archive Edition.)

---

50. Tango Lullaby: A Portrait of Mlle. Alvarez de Toledo

DATE: 24 April, 1940; Paris

SCORING: Piano; arranged for orchestra (flute/piccolo, English horn, clarinet, bassoon, bells,
           strings) in 1944 by Virgil Thomson; transcribed for cello and piano in 1942 by Luigi
           Silva.

Flavie Alvarez de Toledo in 1947;
courtesy of Mlle. Alvarez de Toledo.

Silva; transcribed for violin and piano in 1947 by Samuel Dushkin.

SUBJECT: Flavie Alvarez de Toledo, the daughter of Yvonne de Casa Fuerte (see portrait no. 47).

(VT) - "A beautiful woman. Even now at sixty you'd think she was thirty-five. Both she and her brother are a rare Spanish type, blonde hair with olive skin. Oh, they are incredibly beautiful. Flavie was about seventeen at the time of the *Tango Lullaby*. She married Jean Pierre Cazelle shortly after that and within the next four years had three children."

SOURCES: Manuscript - 10/7 (P2A); *Portraits I*; *Tango Lullaby for orchestra* (New York: G. Schirmer, 1950); *Four Portraits for Cello and Piano*, transcribed by Luigi Silva (New York; G. Schirmer, 1979); *Three Portraits for Violin and Piano*, transcribed by Samuel Dushkin (New York: G. Schirmer, 1947).

RECORDINGS: NS; FINN; CRI; MHS

---

51.   Invention: Theodate Johnson Busy and Resting

Theodate Johnson, painting by Maurice Grosser, 1938; courtesy of Mr. Grosser.

DATE: 29 April, 1940; Paris

SCORING: Piano

SUBJECT: Theodate Johnson (b. Cleveland, 1907); singer and magazine publisher. A younger
             sister of architect Phillip Johnson. Studied at Wellesley College, made New York
             debut recital at Town Hall in 1934. Performed with the Cleveland Symphony and
             Royal Flemish Opera Company in Brussels. Directed a medical relief command in
             Europe during World War II. Joined the staff of *Musical America* in 1954, became
             owner and publisher in 1960, until 1964.
             (VT 3, pp. 220-221) - Theodate Johnson "was getting to be a singer; and as a bru-
             nette with blazing eyes and a jacket of leopard skin, she was looking operatic abso-
             lutely."

SOURCES: Manuscript (P33); *Thirteen Portraits*

52.   Bugles and Birds: A Portrait of Pablo Picasso

DATE: 30 April, 1940; Paris

SCORING: Piano; arranged for orchestra in 1944 by Virgil Thomson; transcribed for cello and
             piano in 1942 by Luigi Silva.

SUBJECT: Pablo Picasso (b. Malaga, Spain 25 October 1881; d. Antibes, France 8 April 1973).

SOURCES: Manuscript - 10/2 (P52); *Portraits I*; *Bugles and Birds: Pablo Picasso*, for orchestra (New
             York: G. Schirmer, 1944); *Four Portraits for Cello and Piano*, transcribed by Luigi Silva
             (New York: G. Schirmer, 1979)

RECORDINGS: NS; FINN; MHS; CRI

53.   Piano Sonata No. 4 (Guggenheim Jeune)

DATE: 1 May & 2 May, 1940; Paris

SCORING: Piano

SUBJECT: Maugeurite (Peggy) Guggenheim (b. 1898; d. Venice, 1979), niece of Solomon R. Guggenheim. Married artist-writer Laurence Vail in 1922 (divorced, 1930). Introduced to modern art by Marcel Duchamp, opened a London Gallery in 1937 nicknamed "Guggenheim Jeune" by her secretary Wyn Henderson. Opened New York gallery in 1942, Art of This Century.
The following excerpt is taken from *Out of This Century: Confessions of an Art Addict* by Peggy Guggenheim (New York: Universal Books, 1979), pp. 217-218:

During the winter I spent much time with Virgil Thomson. He and Howard Putzel and I used to eat a lot together. Virgil was going to help me arrange concerts in my museum if I ever had one. He gave charming Friday evening parties at which he kept open house. He did a musical portrait of me which was not in the least resembling, but for which I posed quietly for several hours, reading his book, *The State of Music*, which is very smart. I thought it would be nice to marry Virgil to have a musical background, but I never got far with the project.

. . . Virgil left Paris before I did, and when I got to America he was the most famous music critic in New York, and was so well known he told me he never did anything he didn't enjoy. He was quite independent. When I told him I had brought Max Ernst to America and was living with him he made a prize remark. He said, 'Lots of ladies seem to have enjoyed that before.' But I am getting way ahead of events."

SOURCES: Manuscript - 10/16 (P27A); originally published as *Piano Sonata No. 4 (Guggenheim Jeune)* (Elkan-Vogel Company, 1946); copyright reassigned to Virgil Thomson, now published as *Piano Sonata No. 4 (Guggenheim Jeune)* (New York: Southern Music).

RECORDINGS: NS

---

54.   Lullaby Which is also a Spinning Song: A Portrait of Howard Putzel

DATE: 3 May, 1940; Paris

SCORING: Piano

SUBJECT: Howard Putzel (1898-1945); art critic, dealer, gallery director, and advisor. Born in Allenhurst, Pennsylvania; moved to San Francisco, took over his father's lace business in 1913, gave it up for art. Little known about his formal education. Ran galleries in San Francisco and Los Angeles. Opened Putzel Gallery in Los Angeles in 1936. Associate of Peggy Guggenheim in Paris and New York. Reference: "Howard Putzel: Proponent of Surrealism and Early Abstract Expressionism in America" by Melvin P. Lader; *Arts Magazine* (March 1982; vol. 56, no. 7) 85-96.
(VT) - "Howard Putzel was a museum man from California. I'd known him through Buffie Johnson, the painter [see portrait no. 107]. He lived in Paris and as a matter of fact, it turned out he was epileptic. He was rather elegant about that. We were having dinner one night at a little restaurant and in the middle of it he suddenly stiffened and started to pass out. The nice French people there understood instantly what was happening and carried him out to the sidewalk and laid him down and put a newspaper between his teeth so he wouldn't bite his tongue. In a little bit he came to and I took him back to his hotel, which was not far from there, up to his room, and laid him on his bed and left him. The next day he either came around or called me up to thank me for this and said he was epileptic, you know, and I said, 'Yes, I recognized it.' He said, 'I can't tell when it's coming on.' "

SOURCES: Manuscript - 10/6 (P53); *Portraits IV*

55.   Five-Finger Exercise: A Portrait of Léon Kochnitzky

DATE: 4 May, 1940; Paris

SCORING: Piano

SUBJECT: Léon Kochnitzky, Belgian poet, born in Brussels in 1894, studied there, and in
          Utrecht, and Paris; received a Doctor of Philosophy degree from the University of
          Bologna. Published seven volumes of poetry and a French translation of the Shake-
          speare sonnets. Contributor to *La Revue Musicale*, Paris. Lectured at Ecole Libres des
          Hautes Etudes, New York.
          (VT 3, p. 200) - "He sought from all modern art that which could remind him most
          intensely of past masters."

SOURCES: Manuscript - 10/4 (P35A); *Portraits II*

56.   The Dream World of Peter Rose-Pulham

DATE: 7 May, 1940; Paris

SCORING: Piano

SUBJECT: Peter Rose-Pulham, English photographer and painter; resident of Paris during the
          1930s and 1940s. Peter Rose-Pulham is a recurring figure in the autobiography of
          Theodora Fitzgibbon, *Love Lies a Loss* (London: Century, 1985). Quoted below is an
          excerpt from *The Times of London* review of the Fitzgibbon autobiography:

          They [Rose-Pulham and Fitzgibbon] lived in unfurnished, unheated rooms,
          often existing on dried bread rubbed with garlic when Peter had pinched the

last few francs to buy paint, but the intellectual atmosphere was heady. He introduced her to Ernst, Cocteau, Giacometti, Dali, and Picasso - who said she had beautiful arms. — Shirley Lowe, "Love and the intellectual moll" (*The Times of London*, Friday, February 15, 1985).

SOURCES: Manuscript - 10/3 (P56A); *Portraits III*
RECORDINGS: MHS

---

57. Dora Maar, or The Presence of Pablo Picasso

DATE: 8 May, 1940; Paris

SCORING: Piano

SUBJECT: Dora Maar, painter, photographer. Born Dora Markovitch; raised in France, daughter of French mother and Yugoslav father. Shortened her name to Maar. Companion to Picasso from 1936-45. Subject of six important Picasso portraits. Dora Maar recorded Picasso's work on *Guernica* (1937) in a famous series of photographs. Excerpt from Roland Penrose, *Picasso: His Life and Work* (New York: Icon Editions-Harper & Row, 1973), p. 298:

At St Germain-des-Prés early in the year [1936], Paul Eluard had introduced to Picasso a young girl with black hair and dark and beautiful eyes who was a friend of his and of the poet Georges Bataille. Her quick decisive speech and low-pitched voice were an immediate indication of character and intelligence. She was a painter and an experienced photographer and had found her way into surrealist circles because of her interest in their work and their revolutionary attitude to life.

(VT) - "Dora Maar was the only one of Picasso's girlfriends who was also what you might call a 'lady.' She was a woman of good education, a good family, a professional in her own right. She was a painter and a photographer. She could also write a bit. Picasso treated her like a lady. But she left, or he moved on to somebody else, as he sometimes did. He gave her her own portrait, which was an enormous gift because by that time, that was the late 1940s, his paintings were worth a great deal of money.

When I did Dora Maar's portrait, she came over to my place and Picasso came along, out of curiosity, I think, and he just sat there. Obviously he got into the portrait! So strong a character couldn't be in a room without being noticed."

SOURCES: Manuscript - 10/3 (P40); *Thirteen Portraits*

---

58.   Pastorale: A Portrait of Tristan Tzara

DATE: 9 May, 1940; Paris

SCORING: Piano

SUBJECT: Tristan Tzara, (b. Rumania, 1896; d. Paris, 1963), pseudonym for Sami Rosenstock, French-language poet and critic. One of the founders, in 1916, of the Dada movement, in Zürich; moved to Paris in 1919. (VT 3, p. 58) - "Tzara said that all art was 'a private bell for inexplicable needs.' "
(VT) - "Rumanian Jewish. One of the original Dadaists. His portrait [a pastorale] just came out that way, like one of those Bach pastorales in 6/8 time."

SOURCES: Manuscript - 10/6 (P67); *Nine Portraits*

---

59.   Aria: A Portrait of Germaine Hugnet

DATE: 12 May, 1940; Paris

SCORING: Piano

Germaine Hugnet, 1935; photo by
Man Ray, copyright Juliet Man Ray,
1985. (From the collection of Mme.
Germaine Hugnet.)

SUBJECT: Germaine Hugnet, first wife of writer Georges Hugnet (see portrait no. 3 for a de-
scription of Georges Hugnet).
(VT) - "Germaine Hugnet. She still exists. She was the first wife of Georges Hugnet.
There was a second wife who also exists, the widow named Myrtille. Germaine was a
solid character and this was the way she came out, as a canon."
The following is a letter sent to the author by Madame Germaine Hugnet, dated 28
October, 1984:

> I have been on friendly terms with Virgil since 1933, the year when I first met
> my husband, Georges Hugnet, who had been a close friend of Virgil for many
> years already. I remember well the evenings and even nights we spent in his
> studio, quai Voltaire, where he received his friends once a week: musicians,
> poets, painters, sculptors—Virgil had always something delicious to offer in
> order to please his friends. We always had much pleasure. I also remember our
> walks in Parc Monceau, where we admired the sculptures, portraits of musi-
> cians.
>   There were also the evenings at the home of Cliquet-Pleyel where Marthe-
> Marthine would sing poems by Georges Hugnet, composed by Virgil. Her
> husband, a composer himself, accompanied her at the piano. I have so many
> charming souvenirs of Virgil.
>   Unfortunately, I am unable to remember exactly the years from 1933 until
> the German occupation, but Virgil will certainly be able to tell you."

SOURCES: Manuscript - 10/2 (P31B); *Portraits II*

60.   Toccata: A Portrait of Mary Widney

DATE: 13 May, 1940; Paris

SCORING: Piano

SUBJECT: (VT) - "Mary Widney was a thin girl from Chicago. She and her husband, Bill, lived
a long time in Paris and when the Germans came in they decided to stay on. I think
that was her decision. She was what we called an 'amateur de sensations fortes.' She
liked strong experiences and she thought that the arrival of the Germans would do
fine. Actually, when the Germans started picking up Americans it was Bill they
picked up. They didn't like American women. And particularly they didn't like
them old or ill. Well, she wasn't old but she was awfully thin, and they thought, well,
I don't know what they thought. At any rate, he was put in a concentration camp
near Paris, the one that they put nice, well-to-do Americans in, and she used to go
out and see him every week. Then eventually the war was over and they came back
to live in America. She died in the Chelsea Hotel and he now lives in New Jersey."

SOURCES: Manuscript - 10/7 (P71); *Portraits III*

RECORDINGS: MHS

61.   Awake or Asleep: Pierre Mabille

DATE: 15 May, 1940; Paris

SCORING: Piano

SUBJECT: (VT) - "Pierre Mabille was a doctor with surrealist connections. He may also have been an amateur painter."

SOURCES: Manuscript - 10/2 (P41); *Nine Portraits*

---

62.   Cantabile: A Portrait of Nicolas de Chatelain

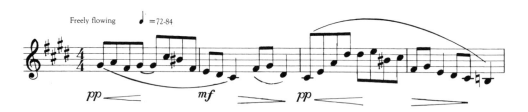

DATE: 29 May, 1940; Paris

SCORING: Piano; arranged for string orchestra in 1944 by Virgil Thomson

SUBJECT: Nicolas de Chatelain (b. St. Petersburg, 1913; d. Paris, 1976), painter, author, journalist. Born to a French Huguenot family in Russia. Became Washington correspondent for *Le Figaro*; Obtained first major interview with Boris Pasternak. Author of *Kennedy and The New Wave*.

(VT) - "Nicolas de Chatelain was of Franco-Russian birth. His father had been French, but I never knew the father, he had been long since dead. His mother was a Russian refugee. He became a painter and he married a very close woman friend of mine, Nonotte Roederer. She came from a French protestant family. When they were married they had three weddings. They had a civil one at the mairie, as you always have to do in France to make it legal. They had one at her mother's house with the protestant preacher and I played Bach on the piano for it, and they had still another one at the Russian cathedral. They remained close friends of mine throughout both lives. She died a little earlier than Nicolas. They had one son who lives in New York, a photographer, works for *Vogue* magazine. Her grandfather was the author of the poem which turned out through various musical ventures to be the *Danse Macabre*. It had been called that as a poem."

(VT 3, p. 315):

On May 29, the day of the bombardment of the Renault factory on the Seine, I was lunching with the Chatelains in Passy, having just composed a portrait of Nicolas, when the sirens sounded. As usual, we did not interrupt ourselves but went on eating while the food was hot, until a gigantic voice said, "Mesdames et Messieurs, go to your shelters." On top of that came the sound of many airplanes and then of explosions. And so we did go down. Ten minutes later, with the all-clear, we went back to eat our peaches, the first of the season.

SOURCES: Manuscript - 10/3 (P18B); *Portraits III*; *Cantabile for Strings: Nicolas de Chatelain* (New York: Mercury Music, 1951), later published by G. Schirmer.

RECORDINGS: FINN; MHS

---

63.   Duet: Clarita, Comtesse de Forceville

DATE: 2 July, 1940; Moumour, Pyrenees

SCORING: Piano

SUBJECT: (VT) - "Clarita de Forceville, formerly a journalist, and her mother were both at Moumour in June of 1940, and it is really a portrait of the two of them, a duet. Her mother, a Venezuelan lady named Madame—or Señora, we called her Madame—Semenario, was the sister of the composer Reynaldo Hahn, who also came from Venezuela."

SOURCES: Manuscript - 10/3 (P24); *Thirteen Portraits*

---

64.   Jamie Campbell: Stretching

DATE: 3 July, 1940; Moumour, Pyrenees

SCORING: Piano

SUBJECT: (VT) - "Jamie Campbell. I hardly knew him. But this was during the summer of 1940 when I was staying with Gertrude Newell who had a house at Moumour down near the Spanish border and several people were staying there. Others would come by, looking for a place to stay or on their way somewhere. I think Jamie stayed around for a week or so and then got off to somewhere else. There was a great deal of moving around at that time. He was somebody that Gertrude had known in New York. He was rather a jolly, pleasant fellow, a man of about thirty. Nothing special about him, and I never knew whether he had a profession or not. He may have had a little money, or he might have been an off-and-on journalist. Anyway, he was there and I did a portrait."

SOURCES: Manuscript - 10/5 (P15A); *Thirteen Portraits*

---

65.   Canons With Cadenza: A Portrait of André Ostier

DATE: 9 July, 1940; Moumour, Pyrenees

SCORING: Piano

SUBJECT: "André Ostier was a French fellow I'd known for a long time and he became, or I guess he'd already become by that time, an excellent, even quite a famous photographer. I never knew him terribly well, but well enough, and he was around with various people I knew. He was a friend of Christian Dior, I remember, also part of a little group of friends."

SOURCES: Manuscript - 10/3 (P50A); *Portraits III*

RECORDINGS: MHS

---

66.   Fugue: A Portrait of Alexander Smallens

Alexander Smallens, 1930s; from the collection of Virgil Thomson.

DATE: 6 September, 1940; Stamford, Connecticut

SCORING: Piano; arranged for orchestra in 1944 by Virgil Thomson

SUBJECT: Alexander Smallens, American conductor (b. St. Petersburg, 1889; d. Tuscon, 1972). Assistant conductor at Boston Opera (1911-23). Music Director of Philadelphia Civic Opera (1924-31), Assistant Conductor of the Philadelphia Orchestra. Conducted the premieres of *Four Saints* and *Porgy and Bess*.

(VT) - "Alex Smallens conducted the summer concerts in the stadium in New York for years, or at least was their principle conductor. He was assistant conductor to Stokowski in Philadelphia. He conducted a great many operas. He had a repertory of over 150 operas. Alex continued to conduct all sorts of tours but the last big thing he did was to take *Porgy and Bess* around the world in the 1950s. He had conducted the first performance of that too. He was a close friend of George Gershwin. He could read orchestral scores like a streak."

SOURCES: Manuscript - 10/4 (P60); *Portraits I*; *Fugue (Alexander Smallens)* for orchestra, available only by rental of orchestral parts from G. Schirmer, New York.

RECORDINGS: CRI

67.   Ruth Smallens

DATE: 15 September, 1940; Stamford, Connecticut

SCORING: Violin solo

SUBJECT: Ruth Smallens. Violinist and composer. Wife of the Russian-born American conductor Alexander Smallens (see portrait no. 66).
(VT) - "Ruth Smallens was Alexander's only wife, but he was her third husband.
She was a musician. She could play the violin and she wrote music sometimes. A
jolly woman. They had a son. As they stayed on being married they quarreled more
and more and she took to drink. Eventually she became quite alcoholic and died
before Alex did."

SOURCES: Manuscript - 7/18 (P61); *Eight Portraits*

RECORDINGS: NS

68.   With Fife and Drums: A Portrait of Mina Curtiss

DATE: 15 June, 1941; Ashfield, Massachusetts

SCORING: Piano

SUBJECT: Mina Curtiss (b. Boston, 1896), author, literary scholar, teacher. Editor and transla-
tor of the letters of Proust. Author of several books, including *Bizet and His World*,
The Midst of Life: A Romance, and a memoir, *Other People's Letters* (Boston:
Houghton-Mifflin, 1978).
(VT) - "Mina Curtiss. Well, that's Lincoln Kirstein's sister. She's a woman of letters
and has written a number of books. She's translated Proust's letters. Earlier, she had
taught at Smith College."

SOURCES: Manuscript 10/7 (P21); *Portraits I*
RECORDINGS: NS; MHS

---

69. Insistences: A Portrait of Louise Crane

DATE: 6 July, 1941; Woods Hole

SCORING: Piano; arranged for band in 1969 by Virgil Thomson under the title *Study Piece: Portrait of a Lady.*

SUBJECT: (VT) - "Louise Crane is un-married, now in her sixties. But I knew her when she was a young girl at Vassar. The Cranes are rich people. They own a paper company in Dalton, Massachusetts which makes not only all sorts of excellent stationary, but the silk-thread paper for the money of the United States. Her grandfather founded the Sheffield Scientific School at Yale. Her aunt, Miss Mabel Boardman, was president of the American Red Cross for many years. Her mother's people are prominent in business, finance, philanthropy. I never knew her father because he was a great deal older and had died. He had been the governor and a senator from Massachusetts [see below]. Louise's mother and brothers I knew well. I still see Louise."
(VT 3, p. 350) - Louise Crane, "a young woman of means who wished to serve music, had undertaken a series of concerts at the Museum of Modern Art, these to include offerings as offbeat as advanced jazz and Yemenite dancing."
Note: Winthrop Murray Crane (1853-1920), father of Louise Crane. Three times Governor of Massachusetts (1900, 1901, 1902); Republican Senator from Massachusetts (1904-1913).

SOURCES: Manuscript - 10/5 (P20A); *Portraits IV; Study Piece: Portrait of a Lady* for band (New York: G. Schirmer, 1972)

70.   Percussion Piece: A Portrait of Jessie K. Lasell

(L.H. tacet)

DATE: 27 September, 1941; Kennebago Lake, Maine

SCORING: Piano; arranged for orchestra in 1944 by Virgil Thomson.

SUBJECT: Jessie K. (Mrs. Chester Whitin) Lasell. (See portrait no. 6 for a detailed description and photo of Mrs. Lasell.)

SOURCES: Manuscript, piano version - 10/6 (P38.1); Manuscript, orchestral version (P38.1A)

71.   Florine Stettheimer: Parades

Florine Stettheimer, 1925; from the collection of Virgil Thomson.

DATE: 5 October, 1941; New York

SCORING: Piano; arranged for orchestra in 1970 by Virgil Thomson, entitled *Metropolitan Museum Fanfare: Portrait of An American Artist.*

SUBJECT: Florine Stettheimer (b. Rochester, 1871; d. New York, 1944), American painter. Studied in New York, Munich, Berlin, and Stuttgart. Scenic and costume designer for first production of *Four Saints*. Shows at Museum of Modern Art, Vassar, and Columbia. Lived with her mother and two of her sisters, Carrie (portrait no. 25) and Ettie (portrait no. 26), until the death of their mother in 1937. Bibliography: Parker Tyler, *Florine Stettheimer: A Life in Art* (New York: Farrar Straus, 1963).
Concerning the title *Parades:*
(VT) - "Well, Florine's studio was a block away from Fifth Avenue and Fifth Avenue is full of parades. It's as if you were always hearing parades going by in the back of your mind."
(VT 3, p. 135) - "Florine was a painter of such high wit and bright colors as to make Matisse and Dufy seem by comparison somber."

SOURCES: Manuscript (P63A); privately printed as "Portrait of Florine Stettheimer," in *View Magazine* (January 1943): 49-52; *Thirteen Portraits*; *Metropolitan Fanfare: Portrait of an American Artist* (New York: G. Schirmer, 1973).

---

72.   The Mayor La Guardia Waltzes

(sketch-orchestra score)

DATE: 2 February, 1942; New York (orchestrated on 3 April, 1942)

SCORING: Orchestra

SUBJECT: Fiorello Henry La Guardia (1882-1947). American political leader. Mayor of New York City during World War II years. (The commission of this portrait, and of no. 73, is described in Chapter IV, p. 44.)

SOURCES: Manuscript, piano sketch -(P36A); manuscript, orchestral version - 4/6 (P36)

73.   Canons for Dorothy Thompson

(sketch-orchestra score)

DATE: 13 March, 1942; New York

SCORING: Orchestra

SUBJECT: Dorothy Thompson (b. Lancaster, New York, 1893; d. Lisbon, 1961). Journalist,
           traveler, political columnist, radio host. Wrote for *New York Herald Tribune, Ladies
           Home Journal, New York Post*. Married three times, to Joseph Bard, Sinclair Lewis,
           and Maxim Kopf. Bibliography: *Dorothy Thompson: A Legend in Her Time* by Marion
           K. Sanders (Boston: Houghton-Mifflin, 1973). (The commissioning of this portrait,
           and of no. 72, is described in Chapter IV, p. 44.)

SOURCES: Manuscript, piano sketches (P65A); Manuscript, orchestral version - 4/5 (P65)

74.   James Patrick Cannon: Professional Revolutionary

DATE: 21 July, 1942; New York

SCORING: Piano

SUBJECT: James Patrick Cannon (1890 - 1974), American Socialist author and organizer.
           (VT) - "James Patrick Cannon was the head of the Trotskyist group in America of
           which the correct name was the Socialist Worker's Party. An old friend of mine from
           college days, Sherry Mangan [see portrait no. 41], had in the 1930s become an addict
           of Trotskyist dogma and started working for the party, which he did for all the rest of
           his life. Anyway, it was Sherry who suggested that I do this fellow Cannon in New
           York and Cannon said O.K., and I went to his office, which was in University Place,
           and sat there and did it and this is what came out. I never saw him before or since."

SOURCES: Manuscript (P16); *Thirteen Portraits*

75.   Peter Monro Jack: Scottish Memories

DATE: 29 July, 1942; New York

SCORING: Piano

SUBJECT: Peter Monro Jack (1897-1944), literary critic and lecturer. Noted scholar and re-
             viewer of poetry, fiction, and biography. Born in Scotland, educated at Cambridge,
             came to the United States in 1927. Wrote for *The New York Times Book Review*, also,
             The Yale Review, The New York Sun, The New Republic. Taught at the University of
             Michigan, Columbia, Barnard, and Sarah Lawrence.

             (VT) - "Peter Monro Jack was a natural born Scottish highlander but he lived in
             America. He had an American wife, he was something of a poet, but he made his
             living in those days not so much by poetry. He was the chief poetry reviewer for *The
             New York Times* and he taught at one of those colleges outside of New York, I think. I
             did this portrait, as a matter of fact, when he was in a hospital and not long before
             he died. He was being very cheerful and we had fun doing the portrait, but he had
             sclerosis of the liver and drank too much Scotch whiskey."

SOURCES: Manuscript - 10/6 (P32); *Thirteen Portraits*

---

76.   Prisoner of the Mind: Schuyler Watts

DATE: 30 September, 1942; New York

SCORING: Piano

SUBJECT: (VT) - "Schuyler Watts was a Yale man with a passion for the theatre; he made some
             good theatrical versions of French plays. He made (edited and arranged) the *Hamlet*
             version that Leslie Howard did." (1936; incidental music by Virgil Thomson; di-
             rected by John Houseman.)

SOURCES: Manuscript - 10/6 (P69); *Nine Portraits*

77.   Wedding Music: A Portrait of Jean Watts

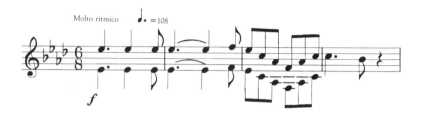

DATE: 1 October, 1942; New York

SCORING: Piano

SUBJECT: Jean Jones, American painter. Married to Schuyler Watts (portrait no. 76) at the
time of this portrait. Married again, H. Sanford Jackson. Used Jean Jackson as her
professional name.
(VT) - "Jean was a painter, a very interesting and charming painter."

SOURCES: Manuscript - 10/7 (P68); *Portraits IV*

Jean Jones Jackson, 1945 (at the time
of this photo, Mrs. Schuyler Watts);
taken for *Town and Country magazine*
in 1945; *courtesy of Mrs. Anne S. Fuller
(sister of Jean Jones Jackson).*

78.   Persistently Pastorale: Aaron Copland

DATE: 16 October, 1942; New York

SCORING: Piano (revised in 1981); arranged for orchestra in 1945 by Virgil Thomson, entitled
            Pastoral: Aaron Copland; included in Thomson's film score for *Tuesday in November*
            (directed by John Houseman) in 1946.

SUBJECT: Aaron Copland, American composer, born December 14, 1900, Brooklyn, NY.

SOURCES: Manuscript, piano - 10/6 (P19A); *Thirteen Portraits*

RECORDINGS: NS

79.   Jane Bowles Early and As Remembered

DATE: 17 October, 1942; New York, and 27 February, 1985; New York. Note from the
            composer regarding the two dates:
            (VT) - "Jane Bowles was composed in 1942. Though fairly long, it had remained
            incomplete. Recently I shortened it a bit and added some material, bringing it to an
            end." - from a letter to the author dated 15 March 1985.

SCORING: Piano

SUBJECT: Jane Auer Bowles (b. New York, 1917; d. Málaga, Spain, 1973), author. Educated at
            Stoneleigh and in Switzerland (private tutors). Married composer and author Paul
            Bowles in 1938 (see portrait no. 29). Settled in Tangier, 1952. Reference: Millicent
            Dillon, *A Little Original Sin: The Life and Work of Jane Bowles* (New York: Holt,
            Rinehart, and Winston, 1981). Also, Jane Bowles, *Collected Works*, Introduction by
            Truman Capote (New York: Farrar, Straus, and Giroux, 1966).

            SOURCES: Manuscript (photocopy-Yale)

80.   Five-Finger Exercise (Portrait of Briggs Buchanan)

DATE: 15 August, 1943; Denville, New Jersey

SCORING: Piano

SUBJECT: Briggs Buchanan (1904-1976); art historian and archaeologist. Close friend of Thomson from Harvard. Fullbright scholar at Oxford. Research Associate at Yale (advisor in Near Eastern Art). Author of *Early Near-Eastern Seals in the Yale Babylonian Collection*, edited by Ulla Kasten (New Haven: Yale University Press, 1981). Enlarged, organized, preserved, and catalogued the Yale Babylonian collection; also catalogued the ancient seal collection at the the Ashmolean Museum in Oxford. Also a member of both New York Stock Exchange.

A recurring figure in Thomson's autobiography, in which many letters to Briggs Buchanan are quoted.

(VT) - "Briggs Buchanan is an old friend from college days. A very devoted friend. He was a stockbroker and did well at it. When he was about forty, he had that under

Briggs Buchanan, 1940s; courtesy of Briggs W. Buchanan, Jr.

complete control and didn't have to pay too much attention to it. So he became an archaeologist. Eventually he was attached to Yale. He is the author of—I think there are three volumes of it—the complete catalog of all the Sumerian seals in the Ashmolean Library, the largest collection in the world, and he invented a way to catalog them. He's extremely well-known in archaeological circles."

SOURCES: Manuscript - 9/9 (P14); "Five-Finger Exercise (Portrait of Briggs Buchanan)," no. 8 of *Ten Etudes for Piano* (New York: Carl Fisher, 1946).

RECORDINGS: FINN

---

81. Solitude: A Portrait of Lou Harrison

Lou Harrison and Virgil Thomson in San Jose, California, 1973, by Pat Meierotto; from the collection of Virgil Thomson.

DATE: 5 December, 1945; New York

SCORING: Piano

SUBJECT: American composer (b. Portland, 14 May 1917). Student of Henry Cowell and Schoenberg. Has written for *Modern Music* and *The New York Herald Tribune*. Also a playwright, conductor, poet, dancer, maker of musical instruments, editor of Ives. (For a description of Harrison, see VT 3, pp. 352-355.)

(VT) - "Lou came to New York about '43, I think. He worked for me for a little bit. He used to come and catalog my music. He also worked for me as a stringer at the newspaper doing extra reviews. He was, in those days, chiefly a twelve-tone composer, but that sort of withered away and his work for the last twenty years or more has been largely centered on the gamelon. He's very knowledgeable about Asiatic music and has had formal lessons in Korea for writing in the ancient Chinese style."

SOURCES: Manuscript - 10/7 (P28); *Portraits I*

RECORDINGS: NS; MHS

---

82. Chromatic Double Harmonies (Portrait of Sylvia Marlowe)

DATE: 17 June, 1951; Newport, Rhode Island

SCORING: Piano

SUBJECT: Sylvia Marlowe, American harpsichordist (b. New York, 1908; d. New York, 1981). A student of Wanda Landowska and Nadia Boulanger. Edited Couperin. Commissioned works from Elliot Carter, Henri Sauguet, Ned Rorem.

Married in 1940 to painter Leonid Berman (d. 1976).

For a remembrance of Sylvia Marlowe, see: "Sylvia Marlowe" (*The New Yorker*, January 11, 1982): 27-29.

Regarding the portrait:

(VT) - "It was like a piano etude because it involved difficult piano fingerings. Afterwards I realized it would work in a volume of etudes."

SOURCES: Manuscript - 9/10 (P43A); No. 7 of *Nine Etudes for Piano* (New York: Carl Fisher, 1954)

RECORDING: NS;

FINN

83. Concerto for Flute, Strings, Harp and Percussion

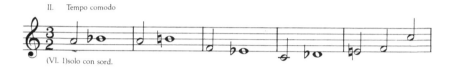

Roger Baker, Westport, 1953 (taken
by Fritz Reiner); from the collection
of Virgil Thomson.

DATE: June-September, 1954; Alcapulco, Mexico

SCORING: Sketched for piano; scored for flute, strings, harp, and percussion. Three movements:
I. Rapsodico
II. Lento
III. Ritmico

SUBJECT: (VT) - "The Flute Concerto is a portrait of the painter Roger Baker. It was sketched on three different days. We were both of us in Mexico, visiting Carlos Chavez. He gave us a bedroom with a two-decker bed and I slept in the lower bed while Roger slept up top. I would compose in my lower bed while he was drawing or something. Anyway, we were in the same room. He wasn't posing consciously, but the three movements of the concerto were his portrait and I knew it at the time. The scoring, naturally, was worked out later."

SOURCES: Concerto for Flute, Strings, Harp, and Orchestra (New York: G. Ricordi, 1957)

RECORDINGS: Louisville Records (LOU S-663), Louisville Orchestra; Whitney (conductor), Fuge (flute soloist).

---

84.   Homage to Marya Freund and to The Harp

DATE: 25 July, 1956; New York

SCORING: Piano; transformed into *Autumn*, Concertino for Harp, Strings, and Percussion, 1964, by Virgil Thomson.

SUBJECT: Marya Freund (b. Breslau, 1876; d. Paris, 1966), Polish-born singer. Specialist in German Lieder and 20th century music. Gave French premieres of Schoenberg's *Pierrot Lunaire*; *String Quarter No. 2*; *Book of the Hanging Garden*. Thomson heard her sing *Pierrot Lunaire* in Paris in 1921, conducted by Milhaud (see VT 3, p. 59).
This work is not a portrait drawn from life, but a piece that Thomson decided after its composition to call a "Homage" to this remarkable singer. However, it is listed in the Yale catalog as a portrait, and is included in the Boosey and Hawkes volume of portraits listed below.

SOURCES: Manuscript, piano version (P25A, P25B); *Thirteen Portraits*; *Autumn*, Concertino for
          Harp, Strings and Percussion (New York: G. Schirmer, 1968).

RECORDINGS: *Autumn*, Concertino for Harp, Strings, and Percussion (1964). Los Angeles
             Chamber Orchestra; Neville Marriner (conductor), Ann Mason Stockton (harp);
             ANGEL S-37300 (1976)

---

85.   For Eugene Ormandy's Birthday, 18 November 1969: A Study in Stacked-Up Thirds

DATE: 18 August, 1958; Tangier
          The manuscript for the version of this piece presented to Ormandy for his birthday
          contains the following inscription: "For the party of 24 January, 1970"

SCORING: Piano

SUBJECT: Eugene Ormandy (b. Budapest, 1899; d. Philadelphia, 1985), conductor of the Phila-
          delphia Orchestra for over thirty-five years.
          (VT) - "This is really a dedication piece rather than a portrait. I can't remember how
          I got it identified with Ormandy, but I did, and I sent it to him as a birthday
          present."

SOURCES: Manuscript - 10/4 (P49); *Nine Portraits*

---

86.   Etude for Cello and Piano: A Portrait of Frederic James

DATE: 18 December, 1966; Pittsburg

Frederic James, 1960s; courtesy of Mr.
Frederic James.

SCORING: Cello and piano

SUBJECT: (VT) - "Frederic James is a painter living in Kansas City. A quite successful painter,
            chiefly of landscapes."
            Quoted below is a letter sent to the author by Mr. Frederic James, dated 10 October,
            1984:

            I have known Mr. Thomson for many years and respect him as a friend and as
            an artist. As you may know, he is a Kansas City native, as am I. At approxi-
            mately the time the "portrait" was done I was in New York, and while there,
            did a number of sketches of Mr. Thomson's apartment which were used in the
            final design of a stage set I designed at the time for the Missouri Repertory
            Theatre.

SOURCES: Manuscript - 7/6 (P32.5)

87.   Edges: A Portrait of Robert Indiana

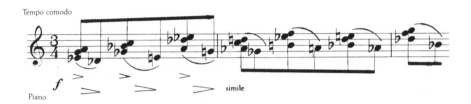

DATE: 24 and 25 December, 1966; New York
The manuscript contains the following inscription: "For his not-on-the-date birth-day party of December 30, 1966/ Virgil Thomson."

SCORING: Piano; arranged for band in 1969 by Virgil Thomson

SUBJECT: Robert Indiana (b. New Castle, Indiana 1928); American painter and visual artist; designed sets for Sante Fe Production of *The Mother of Us All*, 1976.
(VT) - "I've known Robert Indiana for ten years or so. I met him first in the middle 60s, so that makes it nearer twenty years. How'd I know him? In some vague way Andy Warhol was connected with that, whom I knew about the same time, and maybe it was through the pop singer Anita Ellis. But anyway, I've known Indiana for all those years. He has now escaped from New York and gone to live on an island off the Maine coast. But he writes postcards and occasional letters. Bob was a charming fellow and I liked him. Indiana has designed sets for two productions of *The Mother of Us All*. He liked the idea of *The Mother* for some mysterious reason regarding his own birth, I don't know how the connection was made. He was an adopted child and was brought up in Indiana. How he got so attached to *The Mother* I'm not sure. But he actually paid money once for a concert with singers, all doing selections from that opera, at an art gallery where his pictures were on show."

SOURCES: Manuscript, piano version - 10/4 (P31.5); *Edges: A Portrait of Robert Indiana* (New York: G. Schirmer, 1972); *Edges*, arranged for band (New York: G. Schirmer, 1972).

Family Portrait, for Brass Quintet (Portraits No. 88-92)
88. A Fanfare: Robin Smith

DATE: 12 August, 1972; Aspen, Colorado; scored for brass quintet 14 October, 1974.

SCORING: Two trumpets in C, horn in F, two trombones

SUBJECT: (VT 2, Liner notes, Nonesuch Recording) - "*Family Portrait* for brass quintet, consists of five portraits, four of these being members of the same family, the fifth a stranger to the family, perhaps a visitor. All were composed in 1972 and arranged for brass quintet two years later. The family poses were made in Aspen, Colorado; the visitor's took place in New York. The scoring for brass occurred mostly in Jerusalem, where I was a guest of the city in 1974.

Knowing the high skills of the American Brass Quintet, who commissioned the work, I tried to make it quite hard; easy pieces are not what these boys prefer. I also included certain rare instruments which they happen to own — an alto trombone, for instance, and two piccolo trumpets in high B-flat.

In the present group (*Family Portrait*), beneath diversities of character and mood, there seems to be the kind of resemblance that is common to people spending lots of time together. The visitor, on the other hand, has clearly another background, another life. He is from another part of the country too, and quite certainly has other things on his mind."

(VT) - "Priscilla Rea [no. 91] is the daughter of a childhood playmate of mine from Kansas City. Her third husband is the one who is depicted there, named Howard Rea [no. 89]. There are also two daughters of Priscilla's first two husbands: Robin Smith [no. 88] was a child of her first husband, from Houston; Annie Barnard [no. 90], a child of her second. I thought I needed another one and I had Willy's portrait there [Willy Eisenhart, no. 92] and I thought I might just put him in among them as if he were visiting."

SOURCES: Manuscript, piano sketch - 7/10 (P23.5); *Family Portrait* for Brass Quintet (New York: G. Schirmer, 1977)

RECORDINGS: NS

89. Digging: A Portrait of Howard Rea

DATE: 13 August, 1972; Aspen; scored for brass quintet, 13 October, 1974

SCORING: Two trumpets in C, horn in F, two trombones

SUBJECT: Howard Rea (See portrait no. 88)

SOURCES: *Family Portrait* for Brass Quintet (New York: G. Schirmer, 1977)

RECORDINGS: NS

90. At Fourteen: Annie Barnard

DATE: 14 August, 1972; Aspen; scored for brass quintet, 13 October, 1974

SCORING: Two trumpets in D, horn in F, two trombones

SUBJECT: Annie Barnard (See portrait no. 88)

SOURCES: *Family Portrait* for Brass Quintet (New York: G. Schirmer, 1977)

RECORDINGS: NS

91.   A Scherzo: Priscilla Rea

(Alto trombone solo)

DATE: 18 August, 1972; Aspen; scored for brass quintet, 22 October, 1974
SCORING: Two trumpets in D, horn in F, two trombones
SUBJECT: Priscilla Rea (See portrait no. 88)

SOURCES: *Family Portrait* for Brass Quintet (New York: G. Schirmer, 1977)
RECORDINGS: NS

Priscilla Rea, 1984; painting by
Maurice Grosser; courtesy of Mr.
Maurice Grosser.

92.   Man of Iron: Willy Eisenhart

DATE: 23 August, 1972; New York; scored for brass quintet, 22 October, 1974 and 26-27
             January, 1975.

SCORING: Piano; brass quintet—two trumpets in C, horn in F, two trombones

SUBJECT: (VT) - "Willy Eisenhart is a rich young man, no longer really young, from Lancaster,
             Pennsylvania. He recently published a perfectly beautiful book on the American
             painter Donald Evans, who painted little things that look like postage stamps. They
             are very famous and they sell for large amounts of money. Evans died in his thirties
             in a fire in Amsterdam. This book is a collection of his little postage stamp pictures,
             correctly photographed and everything. It has a preface written to it by Willy
             Eisenhart. It's a beautiful book."
             Reference: Willi Eisenhart, *The World of Donald Evans* (New York: Hardin Quist
             Book, 1980)

SOURCES: Manuscript, piano version - 10/6; *Man of Iron* for Piano Solo (New York: G. Schir-
             mer, 1978); *Family Portrait* for Brass Quintet (New York: G. Schirmer, 1977)

RECORDINGS: NS

93.   Bill Katz: Wide Awake

DATE: 15 June, 1981; New York

SCORING: Piano; orchestrated in 1982 by Rodney Lister for inclusion in *Eleven Portraits for Orchestra*

SUBJECT: Bill Katz
            (VT 1) - "A director and decorator of modernistic ballets who has worked in both America and Europe."
            (VT) - "Bill Katz is a tall, handsome young man who makes himself active in the art world and the dance world. He was a close friend and general helper to Robert Indiana [portrait no. 87] and when Indiana got the job of doing sets for *The Mother of Us All* in Minneapolis, Katz was his assistant and went around with him on the job and saw to it that everything got executed as neatly as possible. He has a sense of the stage and some sense of music. Bob Indiana does not understand the stage and does not understand music." [Regarding the title "Wide Awake?"] "His eyes stay open like that."

SOURCES: Manuscript (photocopy-Yale) - 10/2; *Nineteen Portraits*; orchestral version due for publication in 1985 - *Eleven Portraits for Orchestra* (New York: Boosey and Hawkes)

RECORDINGS: SPEC; OSH

---

94.   Norma Flender: Thoughts About Waltzing

DATE: 20 June, 1981; Easthampton, New York

SCORING: Piano

SUBJECT: (VT 2) - "Norma Flender. A New York pianist. Wife of Richard Flender." (See portrait no. 95.)
            (VT) - "The Flenders are my good friends. Dick is a banker. He works for Morgan Guaranty. He's a man of means, with originally, I think, some money from his father. Norma is a pianist; her sister is an actress. Norma keeps practicing, she gives lessons, quite often gives concerts. They have a house of their own in 69th Street and another one at East Hampton, Long Island. I often visit them. And the sister lives in Pittsburg; I visit there. She's married to a lawyer."

SOURCES: Manuscript (photocopy-Yale) - 10/6; *Nineteen Portraits*

RECORDINGS: SPEC

95.   Richard Flender: Solid, Not Stolid

DATE: 21 June, 1981; Easthampton, New York

SCORING: Piano; orchestrated in 1982 by Scott Wheeler for inclusion in *Eleven Portraits for Orchestra*

SUBJECT: Richard Flender; banker, husband of Norma Flender (See portrait no. 94).
             (VT) - "Richard is also a sportsman. He's a skinny little fellow, but he does sport things all the time. Several times a year he either goes out West, or to Switzerland, or to France for skiing. He used to have a ski place of his own in Vermont. He plays golf too and he has a little boat of his own. He's really out for sports."

SOURCES: Manuscript (photocopy-Yale) - 10/7; *Nineteen Portraits*; orchestral version due for publication in 1985 - *Eleven Portraits for Orchestra* (New York: Boosey and Hawkes)

RECORDINGS: SPEC; OSH

96.   Scott Wheeler: Free-Wheeling

DATE: 23 June, 1981; New York

SCORING: Piano; orchestrated in 1982 by Scott Wheeler for inclusion in *Eleven Portraits for Orchestra*; orchestrated for chamber ensemble (fl., Eb cl., Bb cl., bs. cl., piano, perc., vl., va., vcl.) in 1985 by Scott Wheeler (unpublished).

SUBJECT: William Scott Wheeler (b. Washington, D. C. 1952), composer, conductor, pianist. Studied composition with Arthur Berger, Harold Shapero, Malcolm Peyton, and Virgil Thomson. Artistic Director of Dinosaur Annex Music Ensemble in Boston. Music published by Harold Flammer, orchestrations of Thomson by C. F. Peters,

Scott Wheeler, 1983; (photo by Lilian
Kemp); courtesy of Mr. Scott Wheeler

Boosey and Hawkes. Studies at Amherst College, New England Conservatory, and
Brandeis University (Ph.D in theory and composition). Currently an Assistant Pro-
fessor at Emerson College in Boston.
Married in 1985 to Christen Frothingham, an Episcopal minister.
Note submitted to the author by Scott Wheeler, dated 6 February, 1985:

Free Wheeling was written in June of 1981 when I was in New York taking
lessons in text setting and orchestration from Virgil Thomson. He is the only
teacher I've had who would take a pencil to correct not only my orchestrations
but my songs—a bit shockingly "old-school", I thought, but I appreciated his
no-nonsense dispensation of solid professional advice, as well as his generosity
and encouragement.

I like *Free Wheeling*. Not only have I made two very different orchestrations
of it, but I used it as the basis for a short piano piece written as a wedding
present for my sister Jill. She lives in New Mexico, so I called it *Free Ranging*,
and, with apologies to Virgil, I allowed his melody to turn into a thinly dis-
guised version of *Home on the Range*.

SOURCES: Manuscript (photocopy-Yale) - 10/7; *Nineteen Portraits*; orchestral version due for
             publication in 1985 - *Eleven Portraits for Orchestra* (New York: Boosey and Hawkes)
RECORDINGS: SPEC; OSH

97.   Gerald Busby: Giving Full Attention

DATE: 24 and 25 June, 1981; New York

SCORING: Piano

SUBJECT: Gerald Busby (b. Abilene, Texas 1935), composer.
           (VT 2) - "Gerald Busby is a composer of both stage and concert works, notably
           modernistic ballets."
           (VT) - "Gerald Busby is a composer I've known for ten or fifteen years. He lives in
           my hotel right now [the Chelsea]." [Concerning the title, "Giving Full Attention"]:
           "Well, he sits there like that."
           Note sent to the author by Gerald Busby, dated 4 August, 1984:

Gerald Busby (by Tom Victor);
courtesy of Mr. Busby.

The most remarkable aspect of being the object of Virgil Thomson's attention—quite apart from his specific purpose of composing my portrait—was the opportunity he gave me to be myself completely. Like all truly wise people, Virgil simultaneously demands your best and gives you the space to deliver it.

---

98.   Noah Creshevsky: Loyal, Steady, and Persistent

DATE: 26 June, 1981; New York
Score: Piano; orchestrated in 1982 by Virgil Thomson for inclusion in *Eleven Portraits for Orchestra*

Noah Creshevsky, 1981; courtesy of Mr. Creshevsky.

SUBJECT: Noah Creshevsky, composer; studied at Eastman School of Music, State University of New York at Buffalo with Virgil Thomson, L'Ecole Normale de Musique in Paris with Nadia Boulanger, and Juilliard with Luciano Berio. Has had performances throughout the United States, Eastern and Western Europe, Hong Kong, and Japan. Recipient of awards and commissions, including ASCAP Award, and an NEA Composers Fellowship. Currently Associate Professor of Music at Brooklyn College Conservatory of Music of the City University of New York.

(VT) - "Noah Creshevsky was a pupil of mine in Buffalo where in 1963, twenty years ago, I was doing a guest professorship for a half-year. He was one of my students and his family name was Cohen. When he discovered that he was going to be a composer for all the rest of his life, he thought Cohen is just like Smith, so he decided to change it. Not because it was Jewish, because he took another name that was clearly Jewish, the name of his grandfather who had been the original immigrant in the family, Noah Ephraim Creshevsky. He just took that over and he lives by that now. He's a professor at Brooklyn College."

SOURCES: Manuscript (photocopy-Yale) - 10/6; *Nineteen Portraits*; orchestral version due for publication in 1985 - *Eleven Portraits for Orchestra* (New York: Boosey and Hawkes)

RECORDINGS: SPEC; OSH

---

99.   **Sam Byers: With Joy**

DATE: 28 June, 1981; New York

SCORING: Piano; orchestrated in 1982 by Rodney Lister for inclusion in *Eleven Portraits for Orchestra*

SUBJECT: Samuel C. Byers (b. Cameron, Missouri 1950). (VT 2) - "Young, from Missouri, in the advertising business, a fine regional cook."

Note to the author from Samuel Byers, dated 6 August, 1984:

I remember it was a Sunday afternoon at the Chelsea Hotel when Virgil composed my portrait. He invited me up mid-afternoon on that summer day and we sat across from each other at the dining room table. I sat for approximately

Samuel C. Byers; courtesy of Mr.
Byers.

one hour and a half reading James Purdy's *Mourner's Below* while Virgil created my portrait.

The following day Virgil gave me a copy of my portrait, WITH JOY. Gerald
Busby played it for me and my first impression, along with delight, was that I
was riding in a parade in my hometown in Missouri waving to the crowds as
the portrait played repeatedly. Virgil and I share a love of Kansas City, and I
have always thought my portrait captures that love for our home, Missouri.

My love for Virgil Thomson is total and forever.

SOURCES: Manuscript (photocopy-Yale) - 10/7; *Nineteen Portraits*; orchestral version due for
publication in 1985 - *Eleven Portraits for Orchestra* (New York: Boosey and Hawkes)
RECORDINGS: SPEC; OSH

100.   Morris Golde: Showing Delight

DATE: 29 June, 1981; New York

SCORING: Piano

SUBJECT: (VT) - "Morris Golde is a very, very old friend, whose brother has a profitable business making printing machinery. Ever since Morris started making good money he has been a patron of musicians and occasionally of painters. He is a devoted and loyal friend and couldn't be nicer. He does nice things about artists. It was he who published the complete works of the poet Frank O'Hara after Frank's death. As a matter of fact, Frank and I and another fellow were staying with Morris Golde when Frank had his fatal accident."

SOURCES: Manuscript (photocopy-Yale) - 10/7; *Nineteen Portraits*

RECORDINGS: SPEC

Morris Golde; courtesy of Mr. Golde

101.   Christopher Cox: Singing a Song

DATE: 1 July, 1981; New York

SCORING: Piano; orchestrated in 1982 by Rodney Lister for inclusion in *Eleven Portraits for Orchestra*

SUBJECT: Christopher Cox (b. Gadsden, Alabama 1949), Associate editor for Ballantine Books, New York, and a free-lance writer.
            (VT) - "Christopher Cox is a writer. He's a boy from Alabama who works for a publisher in New York and he's still young, about thirty-five, and writing a novel or two. The portrait is a kind of Southern sentimental tune. The Southerness shows up there. He worked for me as a secretary—he's a remarkable typist—at various odd moments when my regular secretary was not there or when I needed two to finish up something."

Christopher Cox (by Dennis
Cooper); courtesy of Mr. Cox

SOURCES: Manuscript (photocopy-Yale) - 10/3; *Nineteen Portraits*; orchestral version due for publication in 1985 - *Eleven Portraits for Orchestra* (New York: Boosey and Hawkes)

RECORDINGS: SPEC; OSH

---

102.   Barbara Epstein: Untiring

DATE: 2 July, 1981; New York

SCORING: Piano

SUBJECT: Barbara Epstein, (b. Boston, 1928); Co-Editor of *The New York Review of Books*. Married Jason Epstein, now divorced; born Barbara Zimmerman. Educated at Radcliffe College.

(VT) - "Barbara and Jason have two children. The son wrote a novel. Barbara does a lot of work around that magazine; she's there all day long every day. The other editor is Robert Silvers."

SOURCES: Manuscript (photocopy-Yale) - 10/2; *Nineteen Portraits*

RECORDINGS: SPEC

---

103.   Dead Pan: Mrs. Betty Freeman

DATE: 11 August, 1981; Corfu (Island off the west coast of Greece)

SCORING: Piano; orchestrated in 1982 by Virgil Thomson for inclusion in *Eleven Portraits for Orchestra, retitled A Love Scene (Anonymous)*

SUBJECT: Betty Freeman, wife of Franco Assetto (portrait no. 105).
Excerpts from a letter sent to the author by Betty Freeman, dated 18 October, 1984:

Betty Freeman, 1984; courtesy of
Betty Freeman.

I was born in 1921 in Chicago, studied music seriously for several years, then
stopped and started being first a producer of concerts at the old Pasadena Art
Museum in the mid-sixties, then became a patron of contemporary music. For
the last ten years of his life I worked with and aided Harry Partch. With Virgil
I have assisted in getting some of his wonderful music on records, especially
The Mother of Us All and *Four Saints*. It's hard to decide between them which is
the best American opera ever written.

Both the musical portraits of me and my husband [see portrait no. 105] were
made on the Greek island of Corfu in 1981 when Virgil was our guest there for
five weeks in the summer. He finished composing a choral work while we went
to the beach each morning. I don't know how he liked being stuck on an
island where the food is terrible—he never said and I never asked. One doesn't
ask Virgil silly questions unless you want to get your head chopped off, isn't
that so?

SOURCES: Manuscript (photocopy-Yale) - 10/3; *Nineteen Portraits*; orchestral version due for
            publication in 1985 - *Eleven Portraits for Orchestra* (New York: Boosey and Hawkes)
RECORDINGS: SPEC; OSH

104.   John Wright: Drawing

DATE: 15 August, 1981; Corfu

SCORING: Piano

SUBJECT: John Cushing Wright, painter.

(VT) - "John Wright. He's a painter. I was visiting Betty Freeman [see portrait no. 103] in Corfu that summer and there were two California couples who also come visiting. One couple was John Wright and his wife. He's a painter and they live in Northern California. They are people of means and he is a perfectly good painter. He made a drawing of me while I was doing his portrait.

SOURCES: Manuscript (photocopy-Yale) - 10/5; *Nineteen Portraits*

RECORDINGS: SPEC

John Wright, 1985 (photo by Thomas Wein); courtesy of Mr. Wright.

105.   Franco Assetto: Drawing Virgil Thomson

DATE: 23 August, 1981; Corfu

SCORING: Piano

SUBJECT: Franco Assetto (b. Turin, 1911), artist; husband of Betty Freeman (see portrait no.
           103).
           (VT 2) - "Italian, primarily a sculptor, but also a painter. The composition of this
           portrait, like those of John Wright and Buffie Johnson, took place while the artist
           was sketching the composer."
           Excerpts from a letter sent to the author by Betty Freeman, dated 18 October, 1984:

Franco Assetto, 1983; courtesy of
Betty Freeman.

Franco Assetto, born in 1911, is an artist who was born and raised in Turin. He is a painter, a sculptor, a fountain maker, an architect, a jeweler—truly a Renaissance man. He loves Virgil. He is as energetic and explosive as V's portrait of him and has great gusto for life.

SOURCES: Manuscript (photocopy-Yale) - 10/4; *Nineteen Portraits*
RECORDINGS: SPEC

---

106.   Dominique Nabokov: Round and Round

DATE: 17 October, 1981; New York

SCORING: Piano

SUBJECT: (VT 2) - "Dominique Nabokov is the fifth wife and the widow of the composer Nicolas Nabokov (1903-1978). Young, French, good-looking, energetic, and a talented photographer."

SOURCES: Manuscript (photocopy-Yale) - 10/7; *Nineteen Portraits*
RECORDINGS: SPEC

---

107.   Karen Brown Waltuck: Intensely Two

DATE: 19 October, 1981; New York

Karen Brown Waltuck, 1983 and
David Waltuck, 1983 (paintings by
Maurice Grosser); courtesy of Mr.
Grosser.

SCORING: Piano; orchestrated in 1982 by Virgil Thomson for inclusion in *Eleven Portraits for Orchestra*

SUBJECT: Karen Brown Waltuck, owner, with husband David, of Chanterelle Restaurant on Grand Street in Soho, New York City. Thomson celebrated his eighty-fifth birthday (25 November, 1981) at a party in the Chanterelle restaurant given by the Waltucks. A copy of this portrait was printed on the cover of the dinner menu for this party. (VT) - "They are very generous and very good friends. And they would put out anybody to give me a table. This piece actually is a portrait of the two of them, but only Karen Brown was posing."

SOURCES: Manuscript (photocopy-Yale) - 10/6; *Nineteen Portraits*; orchestral version due for publication in 1985 - *Eleven Portraits for Orchestra* (New York: Boosey and Hawkes); a copy of the piano version of this portrait is rerpinted in the following article: Dorle J. Soria, "Virgil Thomson," *Musical America* (February, 1982): 38

RECORDINGS: SPEC; OSH

108.   Anne-Marie Soullière: Something Of a Beauty

DATE: 14 November, 1981; New York

SCORING: Piano; orchestrated in 1982 by Virgil Thomson for inclusion in *Eleven Portraits for Orchestra*

SUBJECT: Anne-Marie Soullière, a close friend of Virgil Thomson. Thomson met Anne-Marie when he was a guest lecturer at Yale, where she was executive secretary in the School of Music. Presently, the Associate Director of Development for Yale University. Married in 1984 to Lindsey Kiang, an attorney for Yale University. Anne-Marie Soullière's detailed account of the composition of her portrait appears on page 20.

SOURCES: Manuscript (photocopy-Yale) - 10/2; *Nineteen Portraits*; orchestral version due for publication in 1985 - *Eleven Portraits for Orchestra* (New York: Boosey and Hawkes)

RECORDINGS: SPEC; OSH

Anne-Marie Soullière, 1984 (photo by
T. Charles Erickson, Yale University
Office of Public Information);
Courtesy of Ms. Soullière.

109.   Buffie Johnson: Drawing Virgil Thomson in Charcoal

DATE: 30 December, 1981; New York

SCORING: Piano

SUBJECT: Buffie Johnson, painter, born in New York City. Educated at U.C.L.A., Art Stu-
             dents League; Academie Julien, Paris; S. W. Hayter Atelier; studies with Francis
             Picabia. Over thirty-five shows, dating from Peggy Guggenheim's Art of This Cen-
             tury Gallery in the 1940s to the present, including shows at the Whitney Museum
             and Brooklyn Museum. Works in the permanent collections of over 40 museums,
             including Boston Museum of Fine Arts, the Smithsonian Institution, the Whitney
             Museum, the Guggenheim, and the Yale University Art Gallery. For recent refer-
             ence, see: April Kingsley, "The Primal Plants of Buffie Johnson", *Art International*
             (January-February, 1981): 195-203.

SOURCES: Manuscript (photocopy-Yale) - 10/2; *Nineteen Portraits*

Buffie Johnson; courtesy of Ms.
Johnson.

110.   Craig Rutenberg: Swinging

mf cantando ben sostenuto

DATE: 31 December, 1981; New York

SCORING: Piano

SUBJECT: Craig Rutenberg (b. New Haven, 1952), musician, accompanist, vocal coach. Attended Georgetown University, 1970-74. Lived in France and England, 1976-80. Studied with Pierre Bernac. Worked at the Opéra Comique, IRCAM, regularly at Glyndebourne Festival; director of musical studies at Houston Opera since 1980. Currently working on a degree in psychology with the intention of becoming a full-time therapist. Involved with Houston KS/AIDS Foundation. Trained also as a cook and masseur.

SOURCES: Manuscript (photocopy-Yale) - 10/3; *Nineteen Portraits*

Craig Rutenberg, 1983 (by Arthur
Elgort); courtesy of Mr. Elgort.

111.   Paul Sanfançon: On The Ice

DATE: 2 January, 1982; New York

SCORING: Piano

SUBJECT: Paul Sanfançon (b. Grand Isle, Maine 1940); grew up in a French-speaking section of
           Maine near the Canadian border. An anthropologist; presently a Lecturer in Middle
           East and Comparative Religions at the Museum of Natural History in New York.
           Excerpt from a letter sent to the author by Paul Sanfançon dated 9 August, 1984:

           V.T. suggested that I look like a skater in the photo for your book since the
           piece is a skater's waltz. He saw me skating out at the Hampton's a few days
           before he composed the portrait. I must have impressed him with my turns
           and general showing off. So, I had a friend of mine (Olivia Bauer) do this. I
           couldn't find ice at this time of year, but I suppose carrying skates, scarved,
           hatted and all, I look enough the skater.

SOURCES: Manuscript (photocopy-Yale) - 10/6; *Nineteen Portraits*

Paul Sanfançon, 1984 (by Olivia
Bauer); courtesy of Paul Sanfançon
and Oliva Bauer.

112.   Molly Davies: Termination

Tempo comodo

mf

DATE: 8 January, 1982; Chicago

SCORING: Piano

SUBJECT: Molly Davies, film-maker, wife of conductor Dennis Russell Davies (see portrait no. 113). Lived in St. Paul, Minnesota from 1973-80, where she became associated with Film in the Cities, a media center, as teacher, consultant, and, from 1977-79, Chairman of the Board of Directors. Moved to Stuttgart, West Germany in 1980. Produced *Beyond the Far Blue Mountains*, a three-screen simultaneous projection film with an original score by Lou Harrison (see portrait no. 81), first presented at the Venice Film Festival in 1982. Other works include: *Sea Tails* (a three-screen video), and *The Palm at The End of The Mind* (a three-screen film and slide projection).

Molly Davies, 1983; courtesy of Ms. Davies.

(VT) - "Molly Davies. Her family name was Molly Robison. She was married before and has two earlier children, plus one by Dennis. Her parents are rich. Molly makes modernistic movies. She has collaborated with Ricky Leacock from MIT. Molly is pretty and utterly charming."

SOURCES: Manuscript (photocopy-Yale) - 10/6; *Seventeen Portraits*

---

113.   Dennis Russell Davies: In a Hammock

DATE: 9 January, 1982; Chicago

SCORING: Piano; orchestrated in 1982 by Scott Wheeler for inclusion in *Eleven Portraits for Orchestra*, orchestrated for chamber ensemble (fl., Eb cl., Bb cl., bs cl., piano, perc., vl, va., vcl.) in 1985 by Scott Wheeler (unpublished).

Dennis Russell Davies and Molly
Davies; courtesy of Molly Davies

SUBJECT: Dennis Russell Davies (b. Toledo, Ohio 1944), American conductor. Studied at Juilliard with Jean Morel and Jorge Mester. Director of St. Paul Chamber Orchestra (1972-78). Appointed director of Württemberg State Opera, Stuttgart, in 1978. Conducted at Netherlands Opera and Bayreuth. Well known for performances of American music. Has given first performances of many compositions, including works by Cage, Carter, and Rzewski.

Regarding the title of this portrait, Thomson has said:

(VT) - "Dennis wasn't 'in a hammock,' that's just the kind of music it is. He and his wife I composed in Chicago. The orchestra had invited me out in the dead of winter—my, it was so cold you couldn't believe it—and he was playing my three orchestral pictures.* Molly was with him and we were staying in the same hotel. But, he came out that way; it was rather a surprise."

*Three Pictures for Orchestra (1947, 1948, 1952)

SOURCES: Manuscript (photocopy-Yale) - 10/3; Seventeen Portraits; orchestral version due for publication in 1985 - Eleven Portraits for Orchestra (New York; Boosey and Hawkes)

RECORDINGS: OSH

114.   Rodney Lister: Music for a Merry-Go-Round

DATE: 27 January, 1982; New York

SCORING: Piano; orchestrated for chamber ensemble (picc., Eb cl., Bb cl., bs cl., piano, perc., vl., va., vcl.) in 1985 by Scott Wheeler (unpublished)

SUBJECT: Rodney Lister (b. Fort Payne, Alabama 1951), Boston-based composer, pianist and teacher. Grew up around Nashville, Tennessee. Degrees from New England Conservatory and Brandeis University. From 1973-75, lived in England, where he studied with Peter Maxwell Davies, privately and at the Dartington Hall Summer School of Music. Fellow at the Berkshire Music Center at Tanglewood in 1973. Co-founder and co-director (1971-73) of Music Here and Now, a concert series of new music by Boston area composers for the Museum of Fine Arts, and was music coordinator (1976-82) of Dinosaur Annex Music Ensemble. Currently co-director of The Music Production Company in Boston. His teachers aside from Davies include Malcolm Peyton, Donald Martino, Harold Shapero, Arthur Berger, and Virgil Thomson. Has received commissions from Dinosaur Annex Music Ensemble, The Church of the Advent (Boston), Margaret Lee Crofts, The Boston Philharmonic, Joel Smirnoff,

Rodney Lister, 1984 (photo credit: Woolworth's)

the Fromm Music Foundation at Harvard, the Berkshire Music Center, Serge Koussevitsky Music Foundation at the Library of Congress, and The Fires of London. Recipient of grants from WBZ Fund for the Arts, Somerville Massachusetts Arts Council, and the Martha Baird Rockefeller Fund for Music. Currently teaches composition and theory at the preparatory division of the New England Conservatory.

SOURCES: Manuscript (photocopy-Yale) - 10/7; *Seventeen Portraits*

---

115.   Ðona Flor: Receiving

DATE: 2 February, 1982; Caracas, Venezuela

SCORING: Piano

SUBJECT: Flor Blanco - Fombona, friend of Virgil Thomson from Caracas; married in 1972 to Dr. Marcel Roche (see portrait no. 116)

SOURCES: Manuscript (photocopy-Yale) - 10/3; *Seventeen Portraits*

Ōona Flor, 1983; courtesy of Dr. Marcel Roche.

116. Dr. Marcel Roche: Making a Decision

DATE: 6 February, 1982; Caracas

SCORING: Piano

SUBJECT: Dr. Marcel Roche (b. Caracas, 1920), scientist. Married to the late María Teresa Rolando (d. 1970), four children. Married in 1972 to Flor Blanco - Fombona (see portrait no. 115). Presently, Senior Researcher, Instituto Venezolano de Investigaciones Científicas (since 1959), and Head of the Department of Science Studies. Editor of the journal *Interciencia* (since 1976). Educated at St. Joseph's College (Philadelphia), Johns Hopkins Medical School. Has worked at Peter Bent Brigham Hospital, Universidad Central de Venezuela, University of Cambridge, University of Sussex.

Dr. Marcel Roche; courtesy of
Dr. Roche.

SOURCES: Manuscript (photocopy-Yale) - 10/3; *Seventeen Portraits*

---

117.   David Dubal: In Flight

DATE: 3 March, 1982; New York

SCORING: Piano; orchestrated in 1982 by Virgil Thomson for inclusion in *Eleven Portraits for
           Orchestra*

David Dubal; courtesy of Mr. Dubal.

SUBJECT: David Dubal, New York-based pianist, musical director of WNCN radio station in New York. Has recorded some Thomson piano music on a recital album for Musical Heritage Society—"The Piano In America" (MHS 3808). Author of *Reflections from the Keyboard: The World of the Concert Pianist* (New York: Summit Books, 1984)—a collection of conversations with 33 pianists.

Excerpts from a letter sent to the author by David Dubal, dated 25 November, 1984:

I met Virgil around 1970. I was responsible for bringing him to WNCN for a weekly series of "Live Programs" from the Hotel Chelsea. Virgil had various guests, including Paul Bowles, Ned Rorem, and John Houseman, exploring an enormous range of musical matters. The series lasted one year. We remained friends.

For my portrait Virgil took one and one-half hours. His concentration was enormous. I sat ten feet away from him reading the newly published *Virgil Thomson Reader*. He seemed pleased with the work. I am pleased with it, though strangely, I have not yet learned it. Perhaps because I do not think it looks like me. However, the composer does.

SOURCES: Manuscript (photocopy-Yale) - 10/3; *Seventeen Portraits*; orchestral version due for publication in 1985 - *Eleven Portraits for Orchestra* (New York: Boosey and Hawkes)

118.   Cynthia Kemper: A Fanfare

Violin

DATE: 8 May, 1983; New York

SCORING: Violin and Piano

SUBJECT: Cynthia Warrick Kemper (b. Kansas City, 1930).
           (VT 2) - "From Kansas City, Missouri, a mother, a hostess, and something of a
           grande dame"
           (VT) - "Cynthia Kemper is a lady from Kansas City. She came from a very well-to-do
           family and was married to the richest banker in town. She has three children. Good-
           looking, lady of the world, a very nice woman."
           Excerpts from a letter send to the author by Cynthia Kemper, dated 6 August, 1984:

Virgil was a presence in my life long before I actually met him. So many of my
parent's friends were intimately connected with him that he was a household
eminence. I met Virgil for the first time when, as President of the Performing
Arts Foundation in Kansas City, I offered him a commission for a festival we
were doing.

It was love at first sight. I would see Virgil when I came to New York after
that and one occasion during that period is certainly worth mentioning. We
met for lunch and then went to see a Giacometti show at the Museum of
Modern Art. Virgil did a running commentary, some of it specifically about
the art, most of it a marvelous recollection of Paris and all the people surrounding his life and Giacometti's—Gertrude Stein, Alice Toklas, Picasso, et
al. Other people began to listen and gradually a crowd formed behind us—
Virgil totally unaware. When the tour ended, the crowd applauded, to Virgil's
dismay. It was delicious.

When Virgil did my portrait we had dinner afterwards and his comments
were most interesting. I'd have to say, a little like going to a shrink. He said I
"did not make myself available," I was hard to reach, "complicated." "It took,"
he scolded, "a violin and the piano!"

He had talked for some time about doing the portrait and once, when we
were talking, I said, "How about now?" "No," he said, "You don't feel well
enough, we'll wait for the spring." He was right. How he knew I don't know.
But we did wait for the spring and, behold, a fanfare! . . .

When Virgil gave his papers to Yale, he asked me to come along. Yale provided a limousine for our return trip to New York late in the evening. John
Houseman was with us, having delivered the "apotheosis" for his old friend.

Cynthia Warrick Kemper (photo by
Elizabeth Zeschin, © All Rights
Reserved)

John and Joan Houseman were my neighbors when I lived in Malibu. Riding
between those two men of girth, I had first one sleeping head and then the
other on my shoulder. In between their naps, each one in turn would rouse to
reminisce about their times together—the Mercury Theatre, *Four Saints*, etc. It
was a running account of the history of the arts in America, in a way.

SOURCES: Manuscript (composer; xerox-Yale); *Five Ladies*

---

119.   Peter McWilliams: Firmly Spontaneous

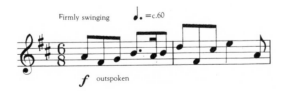

DATE: 11 May, 1983; New York

Peter A McWilliams; courtesy of Mr. McWilliams.

SCORING: Piano

SUBJECT: Peter A McWilliams (b. Detroit, 1949), author, columnist. Author of nine published volumes of poetry, *How to Survive the Loss of a Love*, *The TM Book*, and a highly successful series of books on computers, including: *The Word Processing Book*, *The Personal Computer Book*, and *The Personal Computer in Business Book*.
           (VT) - "Peter's book on the personal computer sells like mad. He makes a lot of money. He also has a column, syndicated somewhere from Kansas City. He's a poet and author."
           Concerning the title, "Firmly Spontaneous", Thomson said:
           (VT) - "Is that what I wrote down? It will do."

SOURCES: Manuscript (photocopy-Yale); *Seventeen Portraits*

---

120.   Vassilis Voglis: On The March

DATE: 4 July, 1983; East Hampton, New York

SCORING: Piano

SUBJECT: (VT) - Vassilis Voglis is a Greek painter. American, but of Greek origin. He's a man
of around sixty."

SOURCES: Manuscript (photocopy-Yale); *Seventeen Portraits*

---

121.   **Power Boothe: With Pencil**

DATE: 12 July, 1983; New York
SCORING: Piano

Power Boothe, 1984 (by Patricia
Bushby); courtesy of Mr. Boothe and
Ms. Bushby.

SUBJECT: Power Boothe (b. 1945), painter and set designer. Educated at Colorado College (BA, 1967); Whitney Museum Independent Study Program (1968). Six one-artist shows at A. M. Sachs Gallery in New York; also at Institute for Contemporary Art, Boston (1984). Recent set designs include the Music Theatre Group/Lenox Art Center's production of Thomson's *The Mother of Us All*, at St. Clement's Theatre (New York City), Lenox Art Center (Lenox, Massachusetts), Wolftrap Farm Park (Virginia). Grants include: National Endowment of the Arts Grant (1975), and New York State Council Grant (1982).

Excerpts from a letter sent to the author by Power Boothe, dated 9 October, 1984:

I remember being honored to be asked by Virgil to sit for the portrait. I asked if I could do a drawing during the session and he agreed. I came to his apartment in the Chelsea Hotel at the appropriate hour and we sat at the dining room table. He would write music and look at me; I would draw with pencil on paper and look at him. Afterwards, he seemed to be surprised my drawing of him was non-objective. It seemed appropriate to me. He asked me if I thought it resembled him, I said I thought it did. We looked at the music. He said he wanted to hold it for a while; maybe he would make some small changes. I took my drawing with me for the same reasons. In a weeks time we met again and made the exchange.

SOURCES: Manuscript (photocopy-Yale); *Seventeen Portraits*

---

122.   Mark Beard: Never Alone

DATE: 23 July, 1983; New York

SCORING: Piano

SUBJECT: Mark Beard (b. Salt Lake City, 1956), painter; grandson of Mormon pioneers. One-person exhibitions: "Indian Series" at Vincent Fitz Gerald & Company (1982), and "The Figure in Landscape" at The Salt Lake Public Library (1980). Group exhibitions include Graphische Sammlung, Munich, The Whitney Museum, New York, Harcus Gallery, Boston, and Ericson Gallery, New York. Collections (over twenty museum and galleries) include The Whitney Museum, The Metropolitan Museum, The New York Public Library, and the Utah Museum of Fine Art.

Mark Beard, 1985 (photo by
Sebastian Li); courtesy of Mr. Beard

(VT) - "Mark Beard is a painter. He lives around here. His family comes from very high Mormon circles. He's tall and he's incredibly handsome. He has muscles in all the places where you wouldn't think anybody could have them."
(Question) - "Is that why his piece is called 'Never Alone?' "
(VT) - "Oh, he's so good looking, yes. Anyway, he doesn't like to be alone and doesn't have to."

SOURCES: Manuscript (photocopy-Yale); *Seventeen Portraits*

123.   Louis Rispoli: In a Boat

DATE: 5 August, 1983; New York

SCORING: Piano; orchestrated for chamber ensemble (fl. E♭ cl., B♭ cl., bs cl., piano, perc., vl.,
va., vcl) in 1985 by Scott Wheeler (unpublished).

SUBJECT: Louis Rispoli (b. New York, 1950), writer, personal secretary to Virgil Thomson.
Educated at State University of New York at Stony Brook, graduate work at University of North Carolina at Chapel Hill.
Mr. Rispoli's detailed account of the making of his portrait, and his working relationship with Virgil Thomson is reprinted in Chapter III, pages 21-24.

SOURCES: Manuscript (photocopy-Yale); *Seventeen Portraits*

Louis Rispoli, 1984; photo by Danyal
Lawson; courtesy of Mr. Rispoli and Mr. Lawson.

124.   Malitte Matta: In the Executive Style

DATE: 20 August, 1983; Paris

SCORING: Piano

SUBJECT: Malitte Matta. (VT) - "Malitte is the second wife of Roberto Matta, the surrealist painter. She lives in Paris. She has a son and, I think, two daughters and she's a nice woman, an old friend of mine. She's worked for several years at the Museum of Modern Art in Paris. She originally comes from Boston, but for the last ten or fifteen years she has cheifly been in Paris and a part of the modern art world."

Malitte Matta, 1980 (by Martine Franck, VIVA); courtesy of Madame Matta.

Excerpt from a letter sent to the author by Malitte Matta, dated 18 September, 1984:

I was born of a proper Bostonian father (in Colonel Pope's house—now the Harvard Club), an Austrian mother, brought up in as many places as they could reach by land, sea, or air—rather a novelty in the thirties—and later found that designing things quite naturally leads to designing events and institutions. This in turn may lead to curious and delightful friendships of which none is valued more highly than that shared with Virgil Thomson.

SOURCES: Manuscript (photocopy-Yale); *Seventeen Portraits*

---

125.   Glynn Boyd Harte: Reading

DATE: 27 September, 1983; New York

SCORING: Piano

SUBJECT: Glynn Boyd Harte. (VT) - "He's an English painter, a draftsman who specializes in architectural subjects. He's done two portraits of me."

SOURCES: Manuscript (photocopy-Yale); *Seventeen Portraits*

---

126.   Bennett Lerner: Senza Espressione

DATE: 29 September, 1983; New York

SCORING: Piano

Bennett Lerner; courtesy of Mr.
Lerner.

SUBJECT: Bennett Lerner, New York-based pianist. Student of Claudio Arrau, Rafael de Silva,
and German Diez. Masters degree from Manhattan School of Music, where he studied with Robert Helps. Extensive performances of 20th Century American music,
including many first performances by major composers. Concerto and recitals at
92nd Street Y in New York, the Charles Ives Centennial Festival in Washington,
and throughout the United States and Europe. Has recorded a successful record of
American Piano Music (Etcetera Records, ETC 1019) including the first recordings
of two Thomson portraits—his own and that of Phillip Ramey (no. 127).
(Question of VT) - "Why is Bennet Lerner's piece called 'Without Expression?' "
(VT) - "Oh, because he came here to have some coaching in those tangos and his
portrait because he was going to play them and record them in Holland, and I
discovered that he'd never danced much. He had no idea how a tango really moved.
So I had to teach him how to do steady rhythm, and then, as you often have to do
with pianists, I had to teach him not to make 'hairpins' all the time [i.e., crescendos
and diminuendos] and to play it straight."

SOURCES: Manuscript (photocopy-Yale); *Seventeen Portraits*
RECORDINGS: ETC

127.   Phillip Ramey: Thinking Hard

DATE: 2 October, 1983; New York

SCORING: Piano

SUBJECT: Phillip Ramey (b. 1939); composer, music journalist. Studied with Alexander
            Tcherepnin from 1959 to 1963 in Chicago, Paris, and Nice; studied with Jack Beeson
            in New York at Columbia University. His compositions include works for chamber
            ensemble, voice, orchestra, and a large body of piano music including two concerti.
            Also, writer on music for numerous magazines and journals; since 1977 he has been
            the annotator and program editor for the New York Philharmonic.
            (VT) - "Phillip is a composer and writes the program notes for the New York Philhar-
            monic. He's all over town. The best gossip in town! You can often find things out but
            you mustn't ever tell him anything."

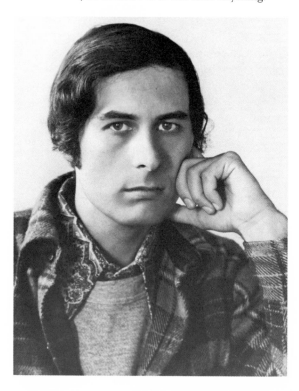

Phillip Ramey; courtesy of Mr.
Bennett Lerner.

From the liner notes to Bennett Lerner's recording of the Phillip Ramey portrait (Etcetera Records, ETC 1019):

When the portrait was finished, Thomson told Ramey, "Your mind is extremely active, as is your body: you fidget. The chords toward the end of the portrait are like you, contradictory."

SOURCES: Manuscript (photocopy-Yale); *Seventeen Portraits*
RECORDINGS: ETC

---

128.   Lili Hastings

DATE: 6 October, 1983; New York
SCORING: Violin and piano; arranged for violin and strings in 1984 by Baird Hastings.
SUBJECT: Louise L. Hastings ("Lili"), French-born, former costume designer, wife of conductor-critic Baird Hastings.
(VT) - "Lili I'm very attached to. She's one of those really nice French women who is so direct and so straight-forward you can't believe it. Baird is a conductor and writes frequent book reviews and occasionally writes a book about ballet and things like that. He was formerly an instructor at Trinity College in Hartford. But for the last eight or ten years he's been in charge of the mechanics of all seven orchestras at the Juilliard School. He's a perfectly nice fellow. Very knowledgeable."
Excerpt from a letter sent to the author by Louise Hastings, dated 17 July, 1984:

I was born in France and until arthritis got the better of me I was a costume designer. In fact, Virgil saw the *Trial by Jury* I designed and my husband conducted. Virgil has been a very long-time friend of my conductor-critic husband and is one of the very most remarkable men I have ever known. I met Virgil at a performance of Dukas' *Arianne et BarbeBleu* at the Paris Opera. We have attended many events together, cooked together, and gossiped together in French and English. I consider *Four Saints in Three Acts* the greatest composition by an American.

As I see him after some four decades of deep friendship, Virgil is a rather wonderful combination of a warm southern gentleman with infinite charm when he wants to use it, particularly with a witty bit of French sophistication

Louise L. Hastings ("Lili") (by Baird
Hastings); courtesy of Mrs. Hastings.

and Harvard learning, *and* a dedicated artist who will be stopped by nothing
to achieve his great work if he can help it.

When I posed for my portrait, Virgil placed me in the dining room of his
very personally arranged Chelsea Hotel apartment. Then he went to work. He
was intense, quiet—writing notes, and sometimes rewriting them, for almost
three hours—often glancing up, I suppose measuring and remeasuring one or
another of the features he perceived. He was calm, but not relaxed. Later,
when I heard the piece, I wondered at his impression of me. Yet several friends
thought they recognized at least two of my qualities—steadfastness and decision, along with an ability to move quickly, on inspiration or need.

SOURCES: Manuscript (photocopy-Yale); information regarding the arrangement of *Lily Has-*
tings for violin and strings by Baird Hastings, can be obtained by writing Mr. Hastings at the Juilliard School of Music in New York.

129.   Charles Fussell: In Meditation

Flowing, neither fast nor slow

mf sempre

DATE: 19 November, 1983; Boston

SCORING: Piano

SUBJECT: Charles Fussell (b. Winston-Salem, North Carolina 1938), Boston-based composer and conductor. Advanced degrees in composition and conducting from Eastman School of Music. Recipient of Fullbright Grant to the Berlin Hochschule, Ford Foundation Grant, and numerous commissions. Has taught at Smith College, North Carolina School of the Arts, University of Massachusetts at Amherst (director of their Pro Musica Moderna), and conducted the Longy Chamber Orchestra. Presently Associate Professor of Composition at Boston University. His works include three symphonies, a choral drama *Julian*, plus chamber scores for various combinations. Mr. Fussell's music is published by G. Schirmer.

SOURCES: Manuscript (photocopy-Yale); *Seventeen Portraits*

Charles Fussell, 1981 (photo by
Kelley Wise); courtesy of Mr. Fussell.

130.   A Portrait of Two, for Joell Amar

DATE: Movement I - finished 8 April, 1984; New York
             Movement II - finished 19 April, 1984; New York
             Movement III - finished 19 April, 1984; New York

SCORING: Oboe, bassoon, piano
             Subjects: Joell Amar (b. Morocco, 1954), bassoonist. Studied at Conservatoire in
             Montreal. Dr. Benjamin Zifkin (b. Montreal, 1951), neurologist, studied at McGill
             University, husband of Joell Amar. Currently living in Brookline, Massachusetts.
             Dr. Zifkin and Ms. Amar commissioned this portrait for performance by Joell
             Amar's trio, Reeds Plus One, a bassoon/oboe/piano ensemble, featuring, in addi-
             tion to Joell Amar, oboist Stella Amar (the sister of Joell), and pianist Yuri Meyero-
             witz (the husband of Stella Amar).
             Joell Amar posed for the first movement of A Portrait of Two, Dr. Zifkin for the
             second movement, and both of them for the third.
             (VT) - "Joell Amar is the wife of a Boston physician, Dr. Benjamin Zifkin. They live
             in Brookline. He is a specialist in epilepsy. He's a very Jewish fellow. He's Canadian
             and she is Moroccan Jewish. And at some point when her family decided that it
             wasn't a good idea to go on being Jewish in Morocco, they looked around the map
             for where it would be nice to move to—they had a bit of money—and they picked
             Canada. It was in Montreal, I believe, that they met and married. Then he got the
             Boston job and there they are."

SOURCES: Manuscript (photocopy-Yale)

131. A Portrait of Jay Rozen *

DATE: 24 April, 1984; New York

SCORING: Bass tuba and piano

SUBJECT: Jay Bernard Rozen (b. Binghamton, New York 1955), tubist. Studied at Ithaca College (BM in Music Education), and Yale School of Music (MM in tuba performance). From 1977-79 was the principal tubist of the Galilee Orchestra in Israel (now defunct). From 1983-84 was employed by the Yale Music Library as an archivist to assist in the processing of the Virgil Thomson Collection. Presently pursuing doctoral studies at North Texas State University in Denton, Texas.

Excerpt from a letter sent to the author by Jay Rozen, dated March 19, 1985:

*May be performed as a prelude to portrait no. 140, *A Short Fugue.*

Jay Rozen, 1985; courtesy of Mr. Rozen.

Because of my involvement with Mr. Thomson's life and music, I thought it would be a good idea to have Mr. Thomson write a work for tuba. When approached on the subject, Mr. Thomson was quite agreeable, and when questioned on the price, he wrote:

'I am meditating a tuba piece.

I have no fixed prices, but like any doctor or lawyer I charge what the traffic will bear.

You might meditate on that.'

Not being able to afford such a commission myself, I thought it would be a good idea to have the piece funded by tubists everywhere. To add incentive, I thought it would be a nice gesture to send donors of fifty dollars or more a copy of the piece personally signed by Mr. Thomson. He agreed readily to this. Anne-Marie Soullière [portrait no. 108] suggested that the commission be sponsored by Yale, thus bestowing upon it the blessing of tax deductibility. Harold Samuel of the Yale Music Library readily agreed to that, and a letter was drawn up and sent to over 250 tubists throughout the world. The response was good. Mr. Thomson suggested that the piece be my portrait, and as I would be joining such illustrious company, I found this an honor I could not refuse. On the 24th of April 1984 I went to the Chelsea and sat for Mr. Thomson.

Subsequently, I placed my letter in the *T.U.B.A. Journal,* and some more money came in. It was then that Mr. Thomson expressed interest in composing a little fugue to go with the portrait. [See portrait no. 140, *A Little Fugue, to follow Jay Rozen's Portrait.*] The premiere of the portrait occurred on October 30, 1984 at North Texas State University during the annual "Octubafest" (Jay Rozen, tuba; Nancy Allen, piano). The premiere of the pair of pieces occurred on March 2, 1985 at the University of Missouri-Columbia as part of the Conference of The American Society of University Composers (Jay Rozen, tuba; Newell Kay Brown, piano). The topic of the three-day conference was "Virgil Thomson: Portrait of an American Composer."

SOURCES: Manuscript (photocopy-Yale)

132.   Brendan Lemon: A Study Piece for Piano

DATE: 4 May, 1984; New York

SCORING: Piano

SUBJECT: Brendan Lemon (b. Yankton, South Dakota 1956). Studied history at the University
of Iowa, and politics and economics at the Institut d'Etudes Politiques in Paris. Currently Vice-President of Caesar Associates, New York.

(VT) - "Brendan Lemon. His portrait was commissioned for him by Peter McWilliams, his friend [see portrait no. 119]. Now, this fellow Lemon turns out to know a
great many of the people I know and he's a writer. I've forgotten what he writes, but
he writes, fiction, I think. He also works as a writer for a firm, writing things that
have to be written in the house, like explanations and all. He does very well and
makes good money. I think it's an easy job, so he gets his own work done too. Good-
looking fellow and perfectly pleasant."

Excerpt from a letter, dated March 27, 1985, sent to the author by Brendan Lemon:

I recollect warmly the day of my sitting. It was the first Friday of May, 1984, a
very rainy afternoon. Prior to the encounter I had been in midtown Manhattan (I'm an associate at a small management firm in Manhattan as well as an
occasional literary critic) where a meeting had run overtime, causing me to
arrive late and somewhat damp at Virgil's Chelsea Hotel apartment. My
friend Peter McWilliams, the poet and computer savant, had arranged the
session, and he was chatting with Virgil when I was ushered into the living
room by Virgil's assistant Lou Rispoli. Peter introduced me to Virgil, and only
a few minutes later Virgil asked him to leave, saying we had work to do.

After asking me a series of questions about myself for about three-quarters of
an hour, Virgil moved us to the dining room. We sat facing each other there,
and while I read Andrew Porter's entry on Verdi in the *New Grove*, Virgil
composed. After an hour or so, the task was completed, and we returned to
the living room for tea and homemade cookies. Then Peter returned, and we
all went off to dinner at Claire on Seventh Avenue.

SOURCES: Manuscript (photocopy-Yale); *Seventeen Portraits*

133.   John Houseman: No Changes

Any speed, but best rather slow

mf   sedately

DATE: 25 June, 1984; Los Angeles

SCORING: Piano; orchestrated in 1984 by Virgil Thomson, *A Pair of Portraits for Orchestra: John Houseman (A Double Take), Anthony Tommasini (Major Chords)*

SUBJECT: John Houseman (b. Bucharest, 1902); director, Academy Award-winning actor, author, educator. Educated in France and at English boarding schools. Director for the premiere production of *Four Saints in Three Acts* in Hartford. Houseman's excellent, detailed account of this production appears in volume one of his memoirs, *Run-Through* (New York, 1972).

SOURCES: Manuscript (photocopy-Yale); *A Pair of Portraits for Orchestra (1984)*, orchestra version - Manuscript (photocopy-Yale)

John Houseman; courtesy of Mr. Houseman.

134.   Lines: for and about Ron Henggeler

DATE: 25 June, 1984; San Francisco

SCORING: Piano

SUBJECT: Ron Henggeler (b. 1953), San Francisco-based artist and photographer. Has taken
over 300 pictures of Virgil Thomson.
Following are excerpts from biographical materials send to the author by Ron Henggeler in January, 1985:

I was born July 12, 1953, 7:07 PM, in Columbus, Nebraska (sun 20 deg. 20
min. Cancer; moon 12 deg. 39 min. Leo; Ascendant 7 deg. 04 min. Capricorn;
and MC 2 deg. 11 min. Scorpio).
    I grew up in Kansas City, Kansas and attended college at Kansas University,

Ron Henggeler, 1984; courtesy of Mr.
Henggeler.

Lawrence, Kansas, majoring in painting and sculpture. In 1974, I moved to San Francisco where I studied painting and sculpture with Tom Phillips, photography with Mark Anstendig, and English composition with John Welsh.

Since its inception, I have worked intensively for The Anstendig Institute and participated in the institute's research on sight, sound, and the vibrational influences on our lives. My posterwork evolved out of my work for the institute. At first, I made posters for the institute's music programs and later conceived the idea of a series of posters each one of which would quote excerpts from the institute's research papers.

I earn my living as a waiter.

SOURCES: Manuscript (photocopy-Yale)

---

135.   **Boris Baranovic: Whirling**

DATE: 21 July, 1984; Camale,

SCORING: Piano

SUBJECT: Boris Baranovic (b. Sibenik, Yugoslavia 1929), theatre designer. Studied art history and theatre design at the University of Naples (1952-56); degrees from Amherst (B.A., 1958) and Yale (M.F.A., 1961). Stage designer for Spoletto Festival from 1965-72. Met Thomson while designing a production of *The Mother of Us All* at Buffalo in 1962. Since 1966, a professor of theatre design at American University in Washington, D.C.

(VT) - Boris Baranovic is a professor of theatre design at American University in Washington. I first knew him when he was doing exactly that at the University of Buffalo when I was being a visiting professor one half year in 1962. He's a "Jug!" (Yugoslav.) And brought up in Italian schools. He speaks beautiful Italian and he knows where all the pictures are in all the museums and churches. Travelling with Boris in Italy is absolute Heaven, because he knows where everything is and what it is.

SOURCES: Manuscript (photocopy-Yale)

136. Anthony Tommasini: A Study in Chords

DATE: 28 August, 1984; New York

SCORING: Piano; orchestrated in 1984 by Virgil Thomson - *A Pair of Portraits for Orchestra: John Houseman (A Double Take), Anthony Tommasini (Major Chords)*

SUBJECT: Anthony Tommasini (b. Brooklyn, New York 1948); Boston-based pianist, musical scholar, and teacher. Educated at Yale University (B.A.; M.M.) and Boston University (D.M.A.). Author of present volume. Currently an Assistant Professor of Music at Emerson College in Boston.

SOURCES: Manuscript (photocopy-Yale); *A Pair of Portraits for Orchestra (1984), orchestral version - Manuscript (photocopy-Yale)*

Anthony Tommasini, 1984 (photo by Lilian Kemp)

137.   Christopher Beach Alone

Tempo commodo

mf   grazioso

DATE: 1 January, 1985; New York

SCORING: Piano

SUBJECT: Christopher Beach (b. Pittsburg, 1951). Educated at Deerfield Academy and Johns
Hopkins University. Formerly Executive Director of Sante Fe Festival Theatre. Currently President and majority stockholder of Earl B. Beach Company.
(VT): "Christopher Beach is a very successful young man of the theatre. He is at
present in business with his father, helping to rescue the family fortunes from disas-
ter."
Excerpts from a letter sent to the author by Christopher Beach, dated March 21,
1985:

> My vitae, Virgil is right, it is the theatre—there never seemed to be a question,
> much less a choice—and now, alas, business and high finance. During my

Christopher Beach; courtesy of Mr. Beach.

years at Deerfield and Hopkins, I ran off for summers to places like Detroit (age 15) and the American Academy of Dramatic Arts. At Hopkins a friend asked if I wanted to help out at the Baltimore Opera running errands. I thought opera was all fat ladies with horns on their heads and big brass bosoms. Somehow two years later I found myself working at the Met as John Dexter's Administrative Assistant. Four glorious years! Then out to Sante Fe. The Festival Theatre was a great idea, my life's ambition, and continues to go strong as it approaches its fifth season. Then we come to Virgil's analysis of saving the family firm and to today.

I guess when I think of Virgil, I think of someone who knows how to hold up his end of a friendship, like his friend John Houseman says on TV, the "old fashioned way." He makes me feel like the center of attention. What I have done is unimportant to him, who I am is all important. Maybe that it why there are many people I see more often, but none I think of more and few who have guided me more through important decisions in my life outside my immediate family than Virgil.

SOURCES: Manuscript (photocopy-Yale)

---

138.   Danyal Lawson: Playing

Danyal Lawson, 1981 (photo by Richard Tamosaitis); courtesy of Mr. Lawson.

DATE: 10 January, 1985; New York

SCORING: Piano

SUBJECT: Danyal Lawson (b. Glendale, Arizona 1953), pianist. Began piano studies in Turkey
            at age of five with Mithat Fenmen, Studied in Japan with Russian pianist Rae Lev.
            Studied in Virginia with Norman Voelcker. Earned Bachelors and Masters degrees
            from Juilliard, student of Miecyzslaw Munz and Josef Raieff. Winner in 1982 of
            Artists International Young Musician's Auditions—New York solo debut at Carne-
            gie Recital Hall. Has performed extensively as solo and chamber music pianist.

SOURCES: Manuscript (photocopy-Yale)

---

139.   Fred Tulan: an Organ Piece

DATE: 24 January, 1985; San Francisco

SCORING: Organ

SUBJECT: Dr. Fred Tulan is a concert organist who has played in 16 countries in a career of 35
            years. He has performed a Virgil Thomson premiere at Westminster Abbey and
            Notre Dame and private recitals for T. S. Eliot and Francis Cardinal Spellman. Has
            played at Oxford, Cambridge, Harvard, Yale, Columbia, Stanford, and University
            of California-Berkeley. Consultant to Edo de Waart and the San Francisco Sym-
            phony on their new tracker and electro-pneumatic organs, Dr. Tulan was heard on
            the televised inaugural and eight 1984 concerts presented by the Symphony, the
            California Bach Society and the American Guild of Organists National Conven-
            tion. Has premiered contemporary works composed for him by Shostakovich, Kha-
            chaturian, Harris, Bliss, Menotti, Castelnuovo Tedesco, Luening, Tansman, Cage,
            Brant and Badings, as well as American premieres of Krenec, Berio, Henze, Schoen-
            berg and Crumb. Virgil Thomson and Fred Tulan have been close friends for over
            twenty years.

SOURCES: Manuscript (photocopy-Yale)

Dr. Fred Tulan, Davies Symphony Hall, San Francisco, 1985 (photo by Glenn Williams).

Virgil Thomson, Davies Symphony Hall, San Francisco, 1985 (photo by Glenn Williams). Courtesy of Fred Tulan.

140.   A Short Fugue: to follow Jay Rozen's Portrait*

DATE: 14 February, 1985; New York
SCORING: Tuba and piano
SUBJECT: Jay Rozen (See portrait no. 131).
SOURCES: Manuscript (photocopy-Yale)

* To be performed with portrait no. 131.

Bibliography

Abraham, Gerald. "Robert Schumann," in *New Grove Dictionary of Music and Musicians.* Sixth edition, edited by Stanley Sadie. London: Macmillan, 1980. (Vol. 16, pp. 831-870.)

Barlow, Samuel L. M. "American Composers, XVII: Virgil Thomson," *Modern Music,* XVIII (May-June, 1941), 242-250.

Bowles, Paul. *Without Stopping: An Autobiography.* New York: Putnam, 1972.

Cage, John and Hoover, Kathleen. *Virgil Thomson: His Life and Music.* New York: Thomas Yoseloff, 1959.

Dillon, Millicent. *A Little Original Sin: The Life and Work of Jane Bowles.* New York: Holt, Rinehart and Winston, 1981.

Dyer, Richard. "Virgil Thomson at 85: Celebrated and Salty," *The Boston Globe,* 29 November 1981, pp. 57, 62.

Garden, Edward. "Anton Rubinstein," in *New Grove Dictionary of Music and Musicians.* Sixth edition, edited by Stanley Sadie. London: Macmillan, 1980. (Vol. 16, pp. 297-300.)

Glanville-Hicks, P. "Virgil Thomson," *The Musical Quarterly,* XXXV, No. 2 (1949), 209-225.

Guggenheim, Peggy. *Out of This Century: Confessions of an Art Addict.* New York: Universe Books, 1979.

Harris, A. S. and Nochlin, L. *Women Artists, 1550-1950.* New York: Alfred A. Knopf, 1976.

Higginbottom, Edward. "(4)Francois Couperin (ii)," in *New Grove Dictionary of Music and Musicians.* Sixth edition, edited by Stanley Sadie. London: Macmillan, 1980. (Vol 4, pp. 860-871.)

Hugnet, Georges. *Fantastic Art, Dada, Surrealism.* Essays by Georges Hugnet, edited by Alfred Barr, Jr. New York: Museum of Modern Art, 1968.

Jackson, Richard. "Virgil Thomson," in *New Grove Dictionary of Music and Musicians*. Sixth edition, edited by Stanley Sadie. London: Macmillan, 1980. (Vol. Vol. 18, pp. 786-789.)

Lader, Melvin P. "Howard Putzel: Proponent of Surrealism and Early Abstract Expressionism in America," *Arts Magazine*, vol. 56, no. 7, (March 1982), 85-96.

McBride, Henry. *Essays and Criticisms of Henry McBride; Selected, with an Introduction by Daniel Catton Rich*. Preface by Lincoln Kirstein. New York: Athenaeum Publishers, 1975.

McVeagh, Diana. "Sir Edward Elgar," in *New Grove Dictionary of Music and Musicians*. Sixth edition, edited by Stanley Sadie. London: Macmillan, 1980. (Vol. 6, pp. 114-130.)

Mellow, James R. *Charmed Circle: Gertrude Stein and Company*. New York: Praeger Publishers, 1974. Avon Books, 1975.

Noble, John. *A Fabulous Dollhouse of the Twenties*. New York: Dover Publications, 1976.

Penrose, Roland. *Picasso: His Life and Work*. New York: Icon Editions-Harper and Row, 1973.

Sanders, Marion K. *Dorothy Thompson: A Legend in Her Time*. Boston: Houghton-Mifflin, 1973.

Stein, Gertrude. *Portraits and Prayers*. New York: Random House, 1934.

Stein, Gertrude. *Two: Gertrude Stein and Her Brother, and Other Early Portraits (1909-12)*. Foreward by Janet Flanner. New Haven: Yale University Press, 1951; reprint ed., Freeport, New York: Books for Libraries Press, 1969.

Stein, Gertrude. *Writings and Lectures: 1911-1945*. Edited by Patricia Meyerowitz. Introduction by Elizabeth Sprigge. London: Peter Owen, 1967.

Steiner, Wendy. *Exact Resemblance to Exact Resemblance: The Literary Portraiture of Gertrude Stein*. New Haven: Yale University Press, 1978.

Thomson, Virgil. *American Music Since 1910*. Introduction by Nicolas Nabokov. New York: Holt, Rinehart and Winston, 1970.

Thomson, Virgil. "Music Does Not Flow," *The New York Review of Books*, December 17, 1981, pp. 47-51.

Thomson, Virgil. "Of Portraits and Operas," *Antaeus* 21/22 (Spring/Summer, 1976), 208-210.

Thomson, Virgil. "Portrait of Florine Stettheimer," *View Magazine*, series 2, no. 1 (January 1943), 49-52.

Thomson, Virgil. "Preface" to *Portraits for Piano: Album One* by Virgil Thomson. New York: Mercury music, 1948; G. Schirmer, 1969.

Thomson, Virgil. "Preface" to *Thirteen Portraits for Piano* by Virgil Thomson. New York: Boosey and Hawkes, 1981.

Thomson, Virgil. *Virgil Thomson*. New York: Alfred A. Knopf, 1966; New York: E. P. Dutton, Inc., 1985.

Thomson, Virgil. Liner notes for *Virgil Thomson: A Portrait Album*. Nonesuch D-79024, 1982.

Thomson, Virgil. *A Virgil Thomson Reader*. Introduction by John Rockwell. Boston: Houghton Mifflin, 1981.

Tyler, Parker. *Florine Stettheimer: A Life in Art*. New York: Farrar Straus, 1963.

Wald, Alan M. *The Revolutionary Imagination: The Poetry and Politics of John Wheelwright and Sherry Mangan*. Chapel Hill: University of North Carolina Press, 1983.

Appendix I:

Index to the Subjects
of the Thomson Portraits

NAME (Catalog Number), page references

Cross References to Subjects Index

A. Portraits: Listed by Titles

B. Portraits: Listed by Scoring
(Chronologically)

109 of the 140 musical portraits by Virgil Thomson are scored for solo piano. Following is a list of the portraits (not including those for solo piano) grouped by instrumental scoring categories. Included are:

a.   the portraits originally scored for diverse instrumental combinations.

b.   the portraits written first for solo piano and later arranged by Thomson for diverse instrumental combinations.

c.   the portraits that are available in published instrumental arrangements by other composers.

Portraits are listed chronologically by scoring category as follows:

Title   *See: (Catalog Number)Name*

SCORING:

Organ

An Organ Piece   See: (139)   Tulan, Dr. Fred

Violin Solo:

Señorita Juanita de Medina accompanied by her mother	See: (1)	Medina, Juanita de
Marthe-Marthine, Madame	See: (2)	Marthe-Marthine, Madame
Poet and Man of Letters	See: (3)	Hugnet, Georges
Cliquet-Pleyel in F	See: (4)	Cliquet-Pleyel, Henri
Miss Gertrude Stein As a Young Girl	See: (5)	Stein, Gertrude
Mrs. Chester Whitin Lasell	See: (6)	Lasell, Mrs. Chester W.

*Now published as *Five Ladies*, (Five portraits for Violin and Piano (New York: G. Schirmer, Inc., 1983)

Tuba and Piano

Orchestra

Appendix II:

General Index

(See Appendix I for Subjects of Portraits)